THE HEJAZ RAILWAY

THE CONSTRUCTION OF A NEW HOPE

THE HEJAZ RAILWAY

THE CONSTRUCTION OF A NEW HOPE

M. Metin Hülagü

BLUE DOME

13 12 11 10   1 2 3 4

Published by Bluedome Press
535 Fifth Avenue, 6th Fl
New York, NY 10017

www.bluedomepress.com

Library of Congress Cataloging-in-Publication Data Available
ISBN: 978-1-935295-03-7

Printed by
Çağlayan A.Ş., Izmir - Turkey

TABLE OF CONTENTS

Part Two
Daunting Challenges to the Railway Construction

Part Three
Stations, Geography, and Rail Lines

Part Four
General Analysis

PREFACE

This book presents a history of the Hejaz Railway based on mainly primary sources in the British archives. One of the few contemporary great powers of the era, the British government was concerned with the construction of railways in Ottoman lands for a number of diplomatic, strategic, and financial reasons. Soon after the British government affirmed the Hejaz Railway Project, British officials began to collect information and write reports on the ongoing project and its progress.

Along the same lines as the general reports, the British Consul or Vice-Consul prepared several confidential reports, which relied on informative data collected on the Hejaz Railway construction particularly by foreigners involved in the construction. For instance, these foreigners included a certain M. Loiso the son of Th. Loiso, the British Vice-Consul at Mersin and an engineer employed in the construction. A few others were Otto von Kapp Kohlstein, the Privy Councilor of the German Emperor and a distinguished engineer of German origin. Kohlstein worked as an inspector of the Lao-Kai-Yutansen line in China and later was a deputy of the High Commissioner of the Hejaz Railway. He inspected the lines from Haifa to Damascus and all the tracks that stretched from Damascus to Ma'an, including the extending lines from Ma'an.

British attachés and other officials, such as Mr. Lloyd, Honorary Attaché to His Majesty's Embassy, carefully worked on a cumulative of such reports obtained from the mentioned and other sources, and compared them with information on the railway, which had been previously available to His Majesty's Embassy.

British reports on the Hejaz Railway were based on various sources, such as British Consuls, Vice-Consuls, and engineers in the field. For the most part, Sir N. O'Conor and Mr. Barclay, a British official serving in Istanbul, sent them to Sir Edward Grey back in London. These reports were compiled in a special file identified as IOR: L/P&S/10/12, and are maintained at Indian Office Library and Records in London. The majority of the sources under scrutiny in this book are these reports. For a list of reporters, including those from consuls and vice-consuls, readers are encouraged to consult the appendices.

Archival sources, the main focus of this book, provide more specific insights into the cultural and technical history of the Hejaz Railway. What seems neglected or not properly reflected on is the diplomatic dimension of it. A more careful and longer study of sources is crucial in order to better understand British diplomacy regarding the Hejaz Railway and its ramifications.

This book, *The Hejaz Railway: The Construction of a New Hope*, consists of four main parts. While Part I deals with the main characteristics of the Hejaz Railway Project and the ways it was put in effect, Part II introduces an analysis of the construction itself. The ensuing Part III focuses more on the results of the construction as far as the officials, laborers, and public were concerned. The concluding section, Part IV, offers an overall examination of the emergence, construction, and launch of the Hejaz Railway and the ways in which it contributed to the broader history of the region.

I hereby acknowledge the great support that Heather Martin gave me during the preparation of this book. Without her help this book would not be possible.

M. Metin Hülagü
Kayseri, Turkey, 2010

INTRODUCTION

Journey of the Locomotive into Ottoman Lands

The early stages of the Industrial Revolution, which began in Britain in the eighteenth century, witnessed the invention of locomotives, which soon proved to be a turning point in the history of many nations around the world. The invention of locomotives further facilitated the advancement of European colonizing nations in Asia and Africa. Scholars in the field note that railways were initially laid near populated areas. Later, the expansion of tracks gave rise to new clusters along the way.

Railways did not only fuel the advancement of European colonizers. The "locomotive" encouraged investors, mainly European, to enter into it as a new, lucrative business that had the potential to grow globally. Soon after, investors considered the Ottoman Empire a venue of business, arguably very productive for both sides.

Railroading inevitably got political. In the second half of the nineteenth century, the British public, particularly those who had the right to vote, did not like the idea of the British government helping the Ottoman Empire build railways, mainly because Ottoman railways would eventually impede British involvement in India and the Middle East. Nevertheless, the concessions that the Ottoman governors occasionally gave to European investors, including those to Britain, made it too profitable to give up railroading in Ottoman lands.

Ottoman Railways

The Ottoman Empire was usually neutral and sometimes benevolent to railroad investors who applied to work in Anatolia or Rumeli. For instance, the railway construction in Rumeli was well underway when the construction of the lines in Anatolia, Izmir to Aydın and Izmir to Kasaba (in Kastamonu), began in 1856. When the first train arrived in Istanbul on 12 August 1888, the opportunity to connect Istanbul through Rumeli to major European capitals, like Berlin, Paris, and Vienna seemed to become plausible[1].

While foreign entrepreneurs wanted to get into the railroading business with the Ottoman Empire for its high profit margins, the Ottoman governors were interested in building a railroad network throughout the Empire in order to consolidate its authority in the regions that were far from the center. They hoped that the railway connections would fortify the state's power across the land; therefore, they gave priority to the farthest and most critical regions in Anatolia and the Arab provinces, like Aleppo, Mosul, Baghdad, Damascus, and Medina. The railway construction that was undertaken in line with this agenda caused numerous regional disputes; however, those involved in the construction were determined to expand the Hejaz Railway to the Holy Lands.

During the reign of Sultan Abdulaziz (1861-1876), the Ottomans laid the groundwork for the line between Istanbul and Anatolia, with the route starting from the Asian side of Istanbul, in Kadıköy, all the way to Pendik in 1871[2]. This line was later extended to Izmit through Gebze. Sultan Abdulaziz launched the line to serve the intensely populated Marmara region and was the first step of a greater railway project extending through Anatolia to Mesopotamia[3]. When this early railway proved too difficult to manage for the Ottoman central government, the Ottoman government assigned its operating rights to a British company in April 1880.

It was later, during the reign of Sultan Abdulhamid II (1876-1909), that full-scale railway projects were put into practice. The lines that were constructed and launched included: Beirut-Damascus, Afyon-Konya, Istanbul-Eskişehir-Ankara, Eskişehir-Adana-Baghdad, and Adana-Damascus-Medina.

---

[1]   For the transformative discourse of railways in the Ottoman context until 1918, see Shereen Khairallah, *Railroads in the Middle East 1856-1948: Political and Economic Background*, (Lebanon: Librairie du Liban, 1991) pp. 42-43.

[2]   Murat Özyüksel, "Hicaz Demiryolu Türkler" in *Yeni Türkiye Yayınları*, vol. XIV (Ankara: 2002), p. 470; and Vahdettin Engin, "Osmanlı Devleti'nin Demiryolu Siyaseti", Türkler, in *Yeni Türkiye Yayınları*, vol. XIV (Ankara: 2002), pp. 464-465.

[3]   Engin, ibid, pp. 464-466.

OTTOMAN RAILWAYS BEFORE THE REPUBLIC

Before the fall of the Ottoman Empire and the establishment of the Repub-lic of Turkey, privately owned European railway companies had already at-tained all the concessions given on railway projects. The companies financed all of their railways in the Ottoman Empire with foreign capital. However, the Hejaz Railway was an exception.

Railway construction, during the late Ottoman Empire, can be catego-rized into two groups. First, there were Ottoman-funded projects, which fo-cused on strategically important regions that resulted in the Hejaz and Bagh-dad railways. Privately funded projects formed the second group, which were in high demand in well-populated regions[4]. They completed the rail lines like Izmir to Aydın and Izmir to Kasaba, Kastamonu. In general, these projects were locally oriented and not undertaken in a coordinated fashion.

What follows is an overview of the Ottoman railways in Anatolia before and after World War One.

OTTOMAN RAILWAYS BEFORE THE FIRST WORLD WAR

1. Izmir-Aydın Line: The Ottoman Empire gave the British a 50-year concession on 22 September 1856 to build and run a rail-way from Izmir to Aydın. Several problems with the ongoing construction delayed the launch of this line until 1866. When launched, it made history as the first railway line to operate in Anatolia and the broader Ottoman domain. The only exception was in Egypt, where the construction of a railway had begun in 1851 connecting Cairo and Alexandria and was completed within five years[5].

2. Izmir-Kasaba Line (also known as Chemins de Fer Smyrne Cassa-ba et Prolongements[6]): A British company secured the concession to construct and operate the line on 4 July 1863. The construction

---

4   Ibid, pp. 464-466.

5   Ibid, p. 462.

6   In the 19th century, specifically the Ottoman Empire in this period, French was *the lingua franca*, a common language applied in engineering. Therefore, railroad terminology origi-nated from French to a large degree.

began the following year and was completed the next year. This line was later connected to the Anatolian railway.

3. Société de Chemins de Fer Ottoman d'Anatolie: The construction of the Ottoman Anatolian Railway Union began in 1873. When it was launched, it connected Istanbul, Izmit, Adapazarı, Eskişehir, Ankara, and Konya.

4. Société Impériale des Chemins de Fer de la Turquie d'Europe: The Turkish Imperial European Railway Union was started in 1874. When completed, the line connected Istanbul to Bulgaria and Greece.

5. Mersin-Adana Line: The line's foundation was laid in 1886 and it joined several Southern Anatolian cities, namely Mersin, Tarsus, Yenice, and Adana.

6. Chemins de Fer de Moudiana à Brousse: The Mudanya-Bursa line construction began in 1892.

7. Transcaucasia Railway: The construction began in 1899 and linked Sarıkamış, Kars, which was on the eastern border, with a 750 millimeter-gauge line, to Erzurum.

8. Société Impériale Ottomane du Chemins de Fer de Baghdad: Construction of the Ottoman Imperial Baghdad Union which began in 1904, passed through Konya, Adana, Toprakkale, Alexandretta, Islahiye, Medyanekbez, Nusaybin, and Baghdad.

OTTOMAN RAILWAYS AFTER THE FIRST WORLD WAR

1. Chemins de Fer de Cilicie Nord Syrie: This line aimed to connect Adana, Toprakkale, Alexandretta, Islahiye, Meydanekbez, Nusaybin, and Baghdad and construction began in 1918.

2. Chemins de Fer d'Anatolie Baghdad: Construction began in April 1924. When completed, the line would connect Istanbul, Izmit Adapazarı, Eskişehir, Ankara, Konya, Pozantı, Adana, and Mersin.

3. Société d'exploitation des Chemins de Fer Bozanti Alep Nissibine et Prolongements: The construction of the line began in 1927 and passed through Adana, Toprakkale, Alexandretta, Islahiye, Meydanekbez, Nusaybin, and Baghdad.

4. Société Turque des Chemins de Fer du Sud de la Turquie (Cenup Demiryolları): On 1 July 1933 construction began and it linked Fevzipaşa, Islahiye, Meydanekbez, Çobanbey, Nusaybin, Payaş, and Alexandretta[7].

From 1856 to 1922, the Ottoman Empire built 8,434 kilometers of railways with funds secured from European sources in Anatolia and Rumeli[8]. Of significant importance, two-thirds of incoming foreign capital was invested in railway projects[9].

Of the 8,434 kilometers of rail lines, 386 kilometers were laid during the fall of the Ottoman Empire and the establishment of the Republic of Turkey. Consequently, a series of treaties signed during this period deprived the fledgling republic of certain railroads. In 1878, the Berlin Treaty disfranchised the mentioned 386 kilometers from Turkish authority; the connection of Eastern Rumeli with Bulgaria disconnected 395 kilometers; as a result of the Balkan Wars, there was a loss of an extra 1,326 kilometers of lines; and the end of World War One culminated in the loss of another 2,526 kilometers. The Republic of Turkey was left with 4,138 kilometers out of a total of an 8,434-kilometer railroad. Furthermore, the quality of the network that remained in Turkish hands was less than adequate. A large section of Anatolia still lacked railways and a number of large cities were not connected via railroad. In 1927, the Turkish Republic State Railways (TRSR) was established to counter these shortcomings. TRSR took over the existing railways in Anatolia and prioritized their modernization and amalgamation into a broader nationwide network. After the establishment of TRSR, the railroads of the Republic of Turkey showed striking improvement in size. Four thousand kilometers of railroad in 1927 increased to 8,500 kilometers, which today does not seem sufficient[10].

The construction of the Hejaz Railroad was beneficial in many respects; however, it invited serious troubles as well. The fierce competition amongst

---

7   For details, see Engin, ibid, pp. 462-469; Khairallah, ibid, pp. 39-40; and the source [available online] at http://www.trainsofturkey.com/history_over.htm (accessed 11/10/2003).

8   Engin, ibid, p. 467.

9   For statistics on the amount invested in Ottoman railroads in 1911, see Khairallah, ibid, p. 39.

10   Online source at http://www.trainweb.org/demiryolu/history_over.htm#BAGHDAD RAILROAD (accessed 10/10/2003).

Britain, Germany, France, and Russia to get involved in the construction caused problems for the Ottoman Empire. In addition, the concessions given in the construction and operation of the lines included a "kilometer guarantee". The foreign contractors who garnered the concessions had the right to claim a certain annual profit based on the kilometer coverage. This would create enormous financial difficulties for the Ottoman administration.

How the Idea Was Born

Planned as a means of convenient pilgrimage transportation to the holy cities of Mecca and Medina, the Hejaz Railway was short-lived, but left a remarkable legacy of the early twentieth century. The railway connected Istanbul, Damascus, Mecca, Medina, and the Red Sea.

The origins of the Hejaz Railway date back to 1864, the year that Dr. Zimpel, an American engineer, proposed the novel project of the railway[11]. Although it was a time of continuous railroad expansion, the Ottoman Empire had to decline his proposal because of its high costs. Moreover, the empire gave the same reason when it rejected similar, subsequent proposals[12].

Sultan Abdulaziz was not able to undertake a series of valuable railroad construction projects. However, such projects were revived in the era of Sultan Abdulhamid II, the last great Ottoman sultan.

Ahmed İzzet Efendi, known later as Arap İzzet Pasha, submitted a project proposal for the construction of a railroad, which was, at the time, considered a vital aspect for modern warfare. As the Endowments and Pious Foundations Governor of Jeddah, Arap İzzet Pasha came up with the most solid and reasonable proposal. The pasha expressed the importance of railways and promoted his idea for the construction of a rail line between Damascus and Medina as a potential way to thwart foreign and domestic threats against the Hejaz Peninsula and Ottoman authority. In addition, the line would facilitate the pilgrimage and maintain territorial and political integrity[13].

---

11   Khairallah, ibid, p. 87.
12   For further analysis, see Ufuk Gülsoy, *Hicaz Demiryolu*, (Istanbul: 1994) pp. 31-40.
13   Ibid, p. 35; Said Öztürk, "Hicaz Demiryolu" in *Osmanlı Devleti'nin 700. Kuruluş Yıl dönümünde Sultan II Abdülhamid Dönemi Paneli II*, (Istanbul: Bilge Yayıncılık) pp. 140-142; and Emine Eyyuboğlu, "Hicaz Demiryolu İnancın ve Emeğin Yolculuğu" in *PTT Dergisi* 27 (Ankara: Ocak 2002): p. 12.

By the time Sultan Abdulhamid II succeeded to the throne, domestic and foreign pressures were overwhelming; particularly, the Europeans' policy of partitioning the Ottoman Empire, which materialized into the broader definition of the Ottoman Empire as "the sick man of Europe". In the face of the insatiable demands proposed by this policy, Abdulhamid II ambitiously predicted that telegraph and rail lines could fortify his central authority by expanding and facilitating communication and transportation across Ottoman territory. Therefore, the sultan approved the Hejaz Railway project, considering that the railway would help improve the defense of the empire against foreign attacks and pave the way for international diplomacy[14]. On 2 May 1900, he issued an imperial edict, *İrade*[15], which sowed the seeds of a decades old dream. As the last of the greatest Ottoman imperial endeavors, "the Hamidiye Hejaz Railway Project", abbreviated as "the Hejaz Railway", went into effect. Consequently, the rail lines were laid from Damascus to Mecca and Medina, the Holy Cities of Islam in the Hejaz region. However, the Ottoman government did not own the lines but classified them as community property in the body of *waqf*[16], the Islamic endowment institutions that recognize the attachment and gratefulness of the world's Muslims.

Along with the Hejaz Railway, the forward-thinking Sultan Abdulhamid II decided to extend other railway and telegraph lines, which were introduced to the Ottoman Empire during the Crimean War. Furthermore, Abdulhamid II gave an executive order in 1900 to join the telegraph lines with the railway that went to Medina. There eventually emerged a number of stations, post offices, and telegraph centers that provided a communication line between Istanbul and Medina[17]. These lines, as well as the Hejaz Railway, brought about formal and informal connections between Istanbul and the Hejaz region.

---

14 Gülsoy, *Hicaz Demiryolu*, pp. 40-41.

15 It is not very well known that an imperial edict was issued to construct a railroad between Syria twenty years earlier. Although a variety of reasons postponed its execution, the idea and determination in building the railroad survived until the end. See L/P&S/10/12, the letter "From Mr. G. Barclay to Sir Edward Grey" Istanbul, 17 November 1906, in the archives *Indian Office Library and Records* [IOR], (London, Political and Secret Department).

16 Özyüksel, ibid, p. 474.

17 Khairallah, ibid, p. 85.

OBJECTIVES

The project aimed to connect Istanbul and Madina and it was believed that the Hejaz Railway would facilitate the pilgrims' journey to the Holy Cities, particularly Mecca. When completed, the Hejaz lines aimed to provide the pilgrims with a more comfortable and safer journey.

The main mode of transportation to the holy cities was the camel caravans. The pilgrimage journey to the Holy Cities could take almost two months, and it was a real challenge even for the sturdiest of pilgrims. Only the distance between Damascus and Medina took 40 days by camel[18]. The journey was excruciating during freezing and very rainy winters and extremely hot summers. The harsh weather conditions were compounded by scattered regional settlements and some armed groups, who exacerbated the conditions of the journey on the way. The figures show that a smaller number of pilgrims, 2,500 to 3,000 of a total 80,000, preferred land travel to the Hejaz. It was assumed that the Hejaz Railway would profoundly change pilgrims' preferences; the rails would be able to bring more pilgrims over land[19].

The successful construction of the Hejaz Railway reduced the travel time of the 1,200-kilometer journey to three days. The travel schedule was set to coordinate with the prayer times. A compartment of the train was assigned as a place of worship and an Imam was appointed to lead the prayers. For four years, from its launch on 1 September 1908 to 1912, the Hejaz Railway safely and comfortably transported 30,000 pilgrims to Medina from distant Ottoman lands. It was not only the pilgrims who rode the trains. According to records, the annual number of passengers rocketed to 300,000, a number that included non-pilgrim passengers as well[20].

The Ottoman administration thought that the railway, alone, would not be able to provide convenient travel and wanted to save the pilgrims from the hardships that resulted from harsh conditions and raiders. Therefore, the Ottoman administration built a series of square forts such as Qasr

---

[18]   FO 78/5452, "Sir Nicholas O'Conor, G. C. B., G. C. M. G.," Damascus, 30 April 1900; also Gülsoy, ibid, pp. 41-43.

[19]   FO 78/5452, "Sir Nicholas O'Conor, G. C. B., G. C. M. G.," Damascus, 30 April 1900.

[20]   Online source at http://nabataea.net/hejaz.html (accessed 16/10/2003); and see Öztürk, ibid, pp. 159-160.

al-Dab'a, Qasr Qatrana, and Qal'a Hasa[21]. Despite all its genuine efforts, the administration was unable to effectively defend the pilgrims against the attacks.

At the time, the Hejaz Railway, the primary way of a comfortable and safe journey to the Hejaz, came to serve the *Surre Alayı*, the annual procession of Imperial Gifts sent to the holy cities of Mecca and Medina. Land caravans had transported the Surre Alayı until 1864. In that year, sea steamers replaced the land caravans. After the Hejaz Railway was launched in 1908, the Surre Alayı changed its method of transportation and, from then on, the trains hauled it.

Despite his wariness of foreigners involved in constructing the railway, Abdulhamid II predicted that the benefits that the Hejaz Railway would present were invaluable. Connecting the pilgrimage route to the holy cities of Mecca and Medina via railroad would facilitate pilgrims' journey to Hejaz and increase the prestige of the caliphate[22].

Religion and religious matters had a favored place among Abdulhamid II's policies in general. This is why he liked to use his title of "caliph" rather than sultan. As a result of such an approach, he particularly wished the line beginning from Damascus to extend as far as Medina. The Hejaz Railroad was one of the most notable projects of the time of Abdulhamid II. In addition, the project held utmost strategic importance; the construction of the Hejaz Railway was a significant attempt to strengthen the Ottoman side against the European powers.

MAKING THE DREAM COME TRUE: THE CONSTRUCTION STARTS

The initiative for the construction of the Hejaz Railway started on 1 September 1900, the anniversary of Abdulhamid II's accession to the throne[23]. A ceremony took place to launch the construction of the line between Damascus and Deraa. In three years, construction reached Amman and Ma'an a year later. Soon after, the operating administration was established and the

---

21 Gülsoy, *Hicaz Demiryolu*, p. 42; also online source http://www.kinghussein.gov.jo/his_ottoman.html (accessed 16/10/2003).

22 FO 78/5452, "From Consul W. S. Richards to Sir N. O'Conor," 10 November 1902.

23 FO 78/5452, "From Consul W. S. Richards to Sir N. O'Conor," 10 November 1902.

transport of passengers and goods started on 1 September 1905. On the same day the following year, construction extended to Medain Saleh and eventually to Medina on 31 August 1908. 1.05 millimeter-gauges were used since they were the cheapest and most suitable lines available[24]. The lines could not be built, as planned, between Medina and Mecca and Mecca and Jeddah, partly because of the high construction costs and partly because some local groups caused too many problems. The failure to complete the project in its entirety affected the realization of political, military, religious, and economic aims in a pernicious way; consequently, the projected goals were not met[25].

During the years between 1900 and 1908, the Hejaz Railway witnessed the construction of 1,464 kilometers of lines. The addition of other lines, like those constructed by the Jerusalem branch in 1911, extended the coverage of the Hejaz Railway to 1,465 kilometers between 1910 and 1911; 1,469 kilometers in 1912; 1,518 kilometers in 1913; 1,585 kilometers in 1914; 1,597 kilometers in 1915; 1,750 kilometers in 1916; 1,802 kilometers in 1917; and, finally, to 1,900 kilometers in 1918[26].

All Ottoman railways, except for the Hejaz Railway, were built and operated by foreigners. In this regard, the Hejaz Railway stands out as an exceptional part of the history of the Ottoman railway system. The project was completed by Turkish labor under foreign management[27]. By the year 1904, the payroll for the construction included German engineer Heinrich August Meissner, who was responsible for the technical engineering of the project[28], and 43 other foreign engineers, 17 of whom were Ottoman citizens[29]. The employee list in the construction of the railway in Muslim Holy Cities is far different and Muslim in majority, particularly because the guardians of the sanctity of Mecca and Medina required that the Christian work force not

---

24 Khairallah, ibid, p. 90; and FO 78/5452, ibid, p. 473.

25 Özyüksel, pp. 475-477.

26 Gülsoy, ibid, pp. 211-212.

27 L/P&S/10/12, "From Mr. G. Barclay to Sir Edward Grey (Confidential)," Istanbul, 17 November 1906 in *IOR*; Gülsoy, ibid, pp. 111-113; and Özyüksel, ibid, p. 473.

28 L/P&S/10/12, "From Mr. G. Barclay to Sir Edward Grey," Istanbul, 17 November 1906 in *IOR*; Khairallah, ibid, p. 89; and Gülsoy, ibid, p. 114.

29 Foreign engineers included 12 Germans, 5 Italians, 5 French, 2 Austrians, 1 Belgian and 1 Greek, see Gülsoy, ibid, p. 114; William Ochsenwald, *The Hejaz Railroad*, (The University Press of Virginia, 1980) pp. 32-33; and Khairallah, ibid, p. 89.

proceed further than Medain Saleh. As a result of this requirement, the 300-kilometer rail lines in southern Medina were constructed exclusively by Muslim engineers and laborers. In time, the Ottoman engineers gained more experience in railway engineering and construction; therefore, foreign involvement in the Hejaz Railway's construction began to decrease. Still, the advice and assistance of foreign engineers continued for a long time[30].

Generally speaking, hundreds of workers and railway engineers worked in the construction and the majority of the railroad was built by a multiethnic work force composed of mainly Turkish soldiers, Syrians, and Iraqis. The soldiers who participated in the construction were paid decently and discharged from military service a year early[31]. Turks, Syrians, and Iraqis, who together comprised a workforce of over 5,000 men[32], succeeded in completing the railroad in eight years, despite the fact that disease, overwhelming changes in weather, and poor working conditions cost the lives of hundreds of workers[33].

Construction, maintenance, and patrolling the lines presented enormous difficulties as a result of the tribal hostilities and territorial structure. Before World War I, the armed groups near the construction zone continuously attacked the railroad[34]. With the added complications of overwhelming changes in weather and shortages of water, the result was a serious impediment imposed on the construction. A number of forts were erected at specific distances along the route in order to counter these attacks and sustain the railroad. Over time, the nomadic sub-culture subsided with the development of urbanization thanks to the Hejaz Railway.

In addition to the attacks on the Hejaz Railway, variations in the terrain along the route of the construction imposed serious setbacks. The terrain was often too soft to work, and sometimes sandy or stony. The shortage of water caused workers difficulties, while heavy rainfall flooded the con-

---

30 Ochsenwald, ibid, p. 33; Gülsoy, ibid, p. 114; and Özyüksel, ibid, p. 473.
31 L/P&S/10/12, "From Mr. G. Barclay to Sir Edward Grey (Confidential)," Istanbul, 17 November 1906 in *IOR*; Özyüksel, ibid, p. 473; and Eyyuboğlu, ibid, p. 13.
32 Özyüksel, ibid, p. 473.
33 L/P&S/10/12, "From Mr. G. Barclay to Sir Edward Grey (Confidential)," Istanbul, 17 November 1906 in *IOR*.
34 FO 195/2286, "Charge d'Affairs (J.H.McMahan, Consul in Jeddah)," Istanbul, 17 August 1908; FO 195/2286, "Acting British Consul, Charge de Affaires," Istanbul, 30 July 1908; and Özyüksel, ibid, p. 475.

struction site at times, washed away bridges and banks, and collapsed the lines[35]. The gradients massively changed as well. Near the Dead Sea, the gradient varied from 300 feet below sea level to 4,000 feet above sea level[36]. Despite these complications, the project continued. The lines were supplemented by hundreds of bridges, tunnels, and other facilities. Specifically, construction included a locomotive maintenance center, 2,666 stone bridges and overpasses, seven iron bridges, nine tunnels[37], 96 stations, seven ponds, 37 cisterns, a hospital in Tabuk and Ma'an, small factories in Haifa, Deraa, and Ma'an, a foundry and pipe workshop, as well as a number of warehouses were in service to successfully complete the Hejaz Railway[38].

How Other Countries Approached

Marshal von Bieberstein, the newly appointed German ambassador to the Ottoman Empire, arrived in Istanbul with little hope for the Hejaz Railway project. Germany's lack of confidence in the future of the project was reflected in the discouraging reports Bieberstein sent to the German Foreign Ministry. On the other hand, Britain's diplomatic approach toward the Ottoman Empire, following the Turco-Russian War (1877-1878), significantly changed. Previous British foreign policy, which considered the Ottoman Empire weak, transformed into a new policy: they started to believe that the launch of the Hejaz Railway could fortify Ottoman authority in the regions where the railroad was going to pass. Such a consideration later translated into a British diplomatic concern. British officials tried to prevent Sultan Abdulhamid II's recruitment of domestic labor for the construction. At the time, papers printed in India and Egypt argued that the Ottoman Empire was robbing Muslims of what they

---

35 L/P&S/10/12, "From Sir N. O'Conor to Sir Edward Grey (Confidential)," Istanbul, 12 June 1906 in *IOR*; L/P&S/10/12, "From Mr. G. Barclay to Sir Edward Grey (Confidential)," Istanbul, 17 November 1906 in *IOR*; and L/P&S/10/12, "War Office to Foreign Office," 26 July 1907 in *IOR*.

36 Available online at http://www.railroadtouring.co.uk/body_july-dec_.html#Hejaz (accessed 13/10/2003).

37 On the Damuscus-Mudawwara section alone, there were 462 bridges, 271 aqueducts, and 799 culverts. Including the viaduct, the total number of engineering works was 1,532. See L/P&S/10/12, "From Mr. G. Barclay to Sir Edward Grey (Confidential)," Istanbul, 17 November 1906 in *IOR*.

38 L/P&S/10/12, "From Sir N. O'Conor to Sir Edward Grey (Confidential)," Istanbul, 12 June 1906; and Öztürk, ibid, p. 153.

thought they had given as donations[39]. The papers further prophesied that the Ottoman Empire would never be able to finish such an enormous railway project; therefore, the Muslim community should turn a deaf ear to the Ottomans. Furthermore, Britain banned the carrying of Hejaz Railway medallions as necklaces[40] and successfully opposed the construction of the railway between Ma'an and Aqaba Bay[41]. During the First World War, the Hejaz Railway would be the main target of British attacks mainly because the existence of the railway, under Ottoman control, was in conflict with British interests in the Middle and Far East.

For the British, the Hejaz Railway, which extended through Transjordan to Aqaba, was believed to be a threat to their hegemony in the Red Sea. They came up with an alternative railway construction plan, which proposed connecting the Mediterranean Sea to the Indian Ocean from Haifa Bay through the Jezreel Valley to the Jordan Valley, Arabah, and the Gulf of Aqaba. This plan was in obvious conflict with the French since both British and French construction plans intended to lay their foundations in the Haifa-Acre zone. This conflict precipitated a Franco-British dispute over control of northern Palestine[42]. The French were mainly concerned with protecting their diplomatic power in Syria and Palestine; thus, they firmly opposed the construction of a rail line between Afule and Jerusalem[43].

Despite opposition from the French regarding Syria and Palestine, the British on the Aqaba issue, and some other elements, the Ottoman Empire proved to the European powers that it was capable of undertaking an enormous project like the Hejaz Railway. Financially and technically, the project was a success. Sultan Abdulhamid II, previously underestimated by Britain and France, was soon regarded as a strong, reputable Sultan after the launch of the railway. The completion of the Hejaz Railway worried the European powers to a great extent and hurried them to plot against Ottoman integrity.

After the Young Turks, mainly the members of the Committee of Union and Progress (İttihat ve Terakki Cemiyeti), curbed Sultan Abdulhamid II's legitimate rule on 21 July 1908 and eventually deposed him in April

---

39 Rüştü Paşa, *Akabe Meselesi*, (Istanbul: 1326 [circa 1908]) p.134; Özyüksel, ibid, p. 472.
40 Özyüksel, ibid, p. 472.
41 Özyüksel, ibid, p. 472.
42 Available online at http://www.golan.org.il/article1.html (accessed 17/10/2003).
43 Özyüksel, ibid, p. 476.

1909, the Ottoman Empire drifted into the First World War in support of Germany, against Britain and France.

FINANCING THE PROJECT

Unlike other Ottoman railways that relied on foreign loans, financing the Hejaz Railway project was Muslim by design. Approximately 18 percent of the imperial budget was appropriated for the construction of the railway [44]. An additional eight million pounds was still necessary but Sultan Abdulhamid II, naturally, had no intention of asking for foreign help. The Sultan turned to the people for collecting the remaining sum[45].

In May 1900, Sultan Abdulhamid II donated 50,000 Turkish liras, the first personal contribution to the Hejaz Railway, and announced to all Muslims that the Hejaz Project needed their donations. The response was quite far-reaching: officers, civil servants, merchants, and many other Muslims from all walks of life inside and outside of the Ottoman Empire[46], mainly from Algeria, Sudan, and India, sent considerably generous contributions for the Hejaz Project[47].

Along with voluntary donations, the Ottoman Empire used various fundraising activities for the Hejaz Railway construction. A common example was the payroll deduction imposed on civil servants; in return they received a Hejaz Railway Medallion[48] made from gold, silver, or lead,[49] re-

---

44   Gülsoy, ibid, p. 58; and Öztürk, ibid, p. 148.

45   Available online at http://www.arab.net/saudi/sa_hejazrailroad.htm (accessed 23/10/2003).

46   Khairallah, ibid, p. 89; Gülsoy, p. 65; and Özyüksel, ibid, p. 472; for a list of contributors see Ochsenwald, ibid, p. 66.

47   Gülsoy, ibid, pp. 84-85.

48   Khairallah, ibid, p. 89; Gülsoy, ibid, p. 131.

49   The medals issued on the occasion of the Hejaz Railway were of two types, wearable and non-wearable, in sizes ranging from 26 to 50 millimeters. Most medals were dated 1318 (lunar calendar), while others were issued four year later, in 1322, when the railroad reached Ma'an, and another four years later, in 1826, when the railroad arrived in Medina. The former type of wearable medals were issued in gold, silver, and nickel alloy and were 30 millimeters in diameter. Initially, ribbons that came with the medals were red, approximately 20 to 25 millimeters in width. Those who made large donations received silver medals and when they suggested that they be given ribbons of different colors to distinguish themselves from regular contributors, the silver medals began to be given with green ribbons. Gülsoy, ibid, p. 131; and online source available at http://www.turkishmedals.net/others. htm#Hejaz (accessed 17/10/2003).

spective to the amount deducted. In addition to the medallion, contributors were granted a *berat*, an Ottoman imperial certificate that could be inherited by their heirs, as a form of encouragement and symbol of their donation and contribution to the holy cause. Between the years 1900 and 1908, all these efforts led to the collection of 3,919,696 Turkish liras from Muslims[50].

In the face of the Ottoman Empire's stagnation at the time, a series of taxes were levied in order to finance the Hejaz Railway. For instance, bureaucratic correspondence required the use of stamps; every *ilmuhaber*, an official certificate, was subject to mandatory contributions; and, sacrificed animal skins (during Eid ul-Adha and other occasions) were collected for completing the railway's construction.

Contrary to the common belief that "the construction of the Hejaz Railway was financed and operated entirely by Ottoman subjects" or that "it was constructed totally by local/national finance and assistance", construction was, in fact, financed by a broader Muslim community in different parts of the world. Regardless of their ethnic identity, Muslims resolutely contributed in the form of subscriptions, one-third of the expenses that were required for the construction[51].

The Ottoman government collected donations from Muslims through a subscription company and allocated everything they received to the construction of the railroad. Consequently, the completion of the Hejaz revived the hopes entrusted upon the caliphate.

LAUNCHING THE RAILWAY

A dream came true with the conclusion of the railway's eight years of construction. Despite overwhelming difficulties, the Ottoman Empire finally launched the Hejaz Railway, with approximately 1,464 kilometers of tracks. On 1 September 1908, the 33rd anniversary of Sultan Abdulhamid II's accession to the Ottoman throne, a great ceremony was held, symbolizing the official opening of the Hejaz Railway. Specific opening dates of each line are the following:

Muzeirib-Deraa on 1 September 1901; Deraa-Zerqa on 1 September 1902; Damascus-Zerqa-Amman on 1 September 1903; Amman-Ma'an on

---

50   Khairallah, ibid, p. 88; and Öztürk, ibid, p. 150.
51   Özyüksel, ibid, p. 473; for more on donations, see Ochsenwald, ibid, pp. 79-82.

1 September 1904; Ma'an-Tabuk in late 1906; Tarek-Medain Saleh on 1 September 1907; and Medain Saleh-Medina in September 1908[52].

Expenditure of the Construction

Starting in 1900 in Damascus and ending in 1908 in Medina, the Hejaz Railway's cost reached over 3,000,000 Turkish liras[53]. In 1916, when the railway covered 1,916 kilometers with additional lines and cross-connections, the construction's total cost amounted to almost 4,558,000 Turkish liras, which was equal to 86,602,000 German marks at the time[54].

Mapping the Destinations: the Network and Intersections

The Hejaz Railway passed through rough desert regions, with few spectacular backdrops. The railway followed a longitudinal route within Ottoman territory: a train could run from Damascus to Deraa in the South, continue across Transjordan via Zerqa and Qatrana, pass through Ma'an into northwestern Arabia, and finally reach Medina via Zat al-Haj and Al-Ula.

The Hejaz Railway's main line reached the following cities, districts, and areas: Damascus, Kiswe, Dair Ali, Mismia, Jebab, Khebab, Mehaye, Shakra, Ezra, Khirbet al-Ghazala, Deraa, Nessib, Mafraq, Khirbet al-Samra, Zerqa, Amman, Kassir, Libban, Jiza, Deba'a, Delma, Khan Zebib, Qatrana, Al-Hassa, Jerouf al-Darawish, Uneiza, Ma'an, Ghadr al-Haj, Shefa, Aqaba, Wadi Rassim, Tel Shahm, Ramle, Batn al-Ghul, Mudawwara, Haraat Ahmar, Zat al-Haj, Bir Hermas, Al-Hazim, Makhtab, Tabuk, Wadi Atil, Dar al-Haj, Mustabka, Al-Akhdar, Khamis, Al-Muazzam, Khism Sana'a, Dar al-Hamra, Mutalli, Abu Taqa, Al-Muzhim, Medain Saleh, Al-Ula, Zumurrud, Hadiyya, Hafirah, and Medina. In addition, several extensions connected major coastal cities to inland cities. For instance, Beirut was connected to Damascus, thanks to a 174-kilometer track, which was laid in 1894. In addition, Haifa in Palestine was connected to Deraa in Syria with a 168-kiometer line.

52 Khairallah, ibid, p. 91.
53 Gülsoy, ibid, p. 138; for another cost analysis, see Ochsenwald, ibid, p. 59.
54 Eyyuboğlu, ibid, p. 13.

Supplementary to the Hejaz Railway, the Beirut-Damascus line was constructed in 1908 by Société Ottomane du Chemins de Fer Damas-Hama ET Prolongements as the sub-line of the Tripoli-Damascus-Humus, Haifa-Jerusalem, and Riyaq-Aleppo lines. With the Hejaz Railway and all the other lines, Istanbul was eventually connected to southern territories, such as Syria, Hejaz, and Jordan. Within his lifetime, Sultan Abdulhamid II witnessed the completion of an enormous construction project that laid 5,792 kilometers of rails. [55]

NEIGHBORING THE RAILS: PEOPLES NEAR THE HEJAZ RAILWAY AND THE BEDOUIN WAY OF LIFE

Local peoples living near the Hejaz railroads were mostly Bedouins. Composed of a variety of scattered tribes, the Bedouins lived independently in a nomadic fashion, which was significantly influenced by the role that the surrounding deserts played on their way of life.

For various reasons, such as drastic changes in weather and tribal feuds, the Bedouin population noticeably shrank until the late 19th century, when several waves of Syrian and Palestinian immigrants streamed into Jordan[56].

In social and cultural terms, many smaller towns flourished thanks to the Hejaz Railway. Ma'an in southern Jordan and Zerqa in the north grew into important centers of cultural activity mainly because pilgrims began to visit these cities during their journey. In addition, the areas that the railroad passed through, such as Haifa and Hauran[57], eventually emerged as major urban centers that the region would take pride in.

THE 1916 REVOLT

Areas in southeastern provinces and the Arabian Peninsula, particularly Palestine, went under tremendous military activity during the First World War. Soon after the war broke out, the Ottoman Empire had serious concerns regarding towns with Arabic-speaking majorities, especially the holy cities of

---

55 Engin, ibid, p. 467; the editor of this monograph updated the names of locations, as well.

56 Available online at http://www.balgawi.com/Jordan/History/ottoman.html (accessed 11/10/2003).

57 Özyüksel, ibid, p. 478.

Mecca and Medina, and the main objective of the Ottoman army was to keep the British out of Egypt and the Suez Canal.

On 29 April 1916, the Ottoman army captured Kut-Al-Imara, a city located in eastern Iraq. In December of the same year, the counter-offensive intensified and the British recaptured the city two months later.

The railroads provided a great opportunity to quickly transport the Ottoman army into the Arabian heartland. In particular, it provided the Medina Military Division defending the Hejaz region with provisions and munitions from Damascus. Because the Ottoman Army preferred the railway to other modes of transportation, the *Sublime Porte*, the Ottoman government, assigned more railroad patrols along the Hejaz Railway. Similar to the way it dealt with the security of traveling caravans in the region, the Porte capitalized on the tribal rivalry[58].

Sharif Hussein, the Amir of Mecca, was an influential figure in the region. He declared a revolt in 1916 to establish his rule. The Hejaz Railway would be the most important factor to determine the fate of the 1916 revolt. While the railway first helped the Ottoman Army to enter and dominate the Hejaz, it later became an Achilles' heel that would cripple their defense.

The British agent T. E. Lawrence organized and led the attacks to destroy the lines. Furthermore, Lawrence was also supported by the caravan owners and operators who were threatened by the railway, which offered cheaper, faster, and safer transportation than the arduous, two-month long journey with their camel caravans. For example, the figures from early 1909 show that the travel costs of a pilgrim decreased by 50 percent and the entire convoy composed of northern-bound pilgrim ships, called "pool", carried its freights 50 percent better than those in previous years[59].

Once a symbol of Muslim brotherhood and enterprise, the Hejaz Railway was under frequent attack, severely damaged, and eventually destroyed. The sections of the railway from Ma'an to Jordan and down to Medina were too severely damaged to operate after the war ended in 1918. It took 10 years of restoration to return them to working order. In addition, the telegraph lines between Damascus and Deraa were paralyzed. Consequently, four centuries of Ottoman rule in the region came to an end. As a result of

---

58 Cezmi Eraslan, *II. Abdulhamid ve İslam Birliği*, (Istanbul: 1992) p. 218.
59 FO 424/219, "Sir G. Lowther to Sir Edward Grey," Istanbul, 5 April 1909.

the Sykes-Picot Agreement, which Britain and France signed in a secret meeting, Britain did not keep its promises to Sharif Hussein but, instead, divided the Arab World with France.

Legacy of the Hejaz Railway: The Remains

Famous in the West for the role it played in the First World War and its affiliation with Lawrence, the line that was known as "the Turkish Road" in the Jordan District was left to decay after the fall of the Ottoman Empire.

After the war, the station buildings and water towers turned into ruins, along with the line itself. The rail metals, which had survived under the dry, desert climate and had even been burnished by flitting particles of sand, were disjoined and sold. In some Saudi Arabian cities like Tabuk, where trains used to stop en route to and from the Hejaz, the remnants of the Hejaz Railway remain to this day. These types of remnants and scenes of skirmishes have, also, survived along the route to Medain Saleh, another central station on the railway route.

Article number 360 of the Treaty of Sévres, signed between the Allied Powers and Turkey on 10 August 1920, stipulated that the Turkish Government cease all its claims and rights over the Hejaz Railway, sanction the following arrangements of the railway's operations, and abide to the distribution of the property pertaining to the railway by other, concerned governments. In the end, the article led the governments of Syria, Palestine, and Transjordan to take over administration of the operating sections of the railway.

The initial idea and route of the Hejaz Railway has long been abandoned. Only the surviving sections in Syria and Jordan operate partially. For example, the subsection linking the phosphate mines to the Aqaba Port use a new line, which was built off the old main line. Some of the original locomotives in Syria are tourist attractions during summer.

The lines in Saudi Arabia went out of service and most of its tracks were destroyed. Several station buildings and bridges of the Hejaz Railway project have survived but have quickly decayed due to a lack of interest and maintenance.

The Haifa and Jerusalem stations in the Israeli division were the most important stations on the line. Although they are still standing, they do not operate for obvious reasons. The sections in the Lebanese division, on the other hand, incurred severe damage during the civil war.

Restoring the Railway

Several efforts have been made to restore the Hejaz Railway since the First World War and, as recently as, 1971. They all were doomed to fail. For instance, attempts to reconstruct the line in the 1960s were unable to materialize because the reconstruction plan proved too expensive to commence.

The rapid transformation in aviation technology made the reconstruction of the railway more difficult. In December 2001, the ministers of transportation of Syria, Jordan, and Saudi Arabia met to revive the legendary railway and agreed on an active agenda to pursue the matter. A meeting of technical experts in Damascus followed, with the objective to formulate a plan of action to reconstruct the railway.

In addition, Syria and Turkey discussed ways to restore the lines of the Hejaz Railway between the two countries in mid-1999. However, financial difficulties, already existing and inexpensive passenger rail services from Syria to Jordan, Turkey, and Iran, and the carriage status available with limited schedules were too overwhelming. Despite all these factors, an agreement was signed in 2000 to launch railroad transportation between Gaziantep and Damascus[60].

---

60 Available online at http://members.tripod.com/mirzabeyoglu/secmece153.htm (accessed 13/11/2003).

PART ONE

Overview of the Hejaz Railway
Construction

OVERVIEW OF THE HEJAZ RAILWAY CONSTRUCTION

Brief History of the Construction

The Muslim community had long dreamed of a railway leading to Mecca. For that purpose, İzzet Pasha, the secretary and advisor to the Sultan[1], took the first step. İzzet Pasha led the initiative for a project to connect Damascus with the Holy Cities of Islam by rail, thereby increasing the property value in the Damascus neighborhood[2].

As soon as an Imperial İrade, or Decree, was issued on 1 May 1900, and authorized the construction of the lines, preparations began[3]. The sultan later ordered another irade to adopt means and measures to ensure that the Hejaz Railway project could be completed in the shortest possible period of time[4].

Ottoman Central Administration

Initially, there were a variety of opinions as to whether head offices, factories, and repair centers should be built in Damascus, Deraa, or Haifa. The Hejaz Railroad Board ruled that the line manager had to be in constant contact with the provincial officers, Beirut-Damascus Railroad Administration, and merchants of Damascus. In addition, they thought that local offices and repair centers had to be opened in Damascus. In fact, construction started

---

[1] FO 78/5452, "H.R. O'Conor," Istanbul, 23 May 1900; and L/P&S/10/12, "From Sir N. O'Conor to Sir Edward Grey (Confidential)," Istanbul, 12 June 1906 in *IOR*.

[2] FO 78/5452, "H.R. O'Conor," Istanbul 23 May 1900.

[3] L/P&S/10/12, "From Mr. G. Barclay to Sir Edward Grey," Istanbul, 17 November 1906 in *IOR*; L/P&S/10/12, "From Sir N. O'Conor to Sir Edward Grey (Confidential)," Istanbul, 12 June 1906 in *IOR*.

[4] L/P&S/10/12, "W.S. Richards," Damascus, 8 February 1902 in *IOR*.

with orders coming from the temporary head offices established in Haifa[5]. The equipment and supplies, such as rails, sleepers, and rolling stocks, were shipped to their final destinations from Haifa, where there was a goods manager. In addition, domestic exports were sent to the Port of Haifa after the Deraa–Haifa branch opened. While an assistant to the goods manager was stationed in Deraa, the junction of the two railroads, the works manager was stationed in Damascus, where the largest engine and wagon repair workshops were located. The officers in charge were also in Haifa. Müşir Rıza Pasha, previously an incompetent commander in Yemen, was the nominal manager. Next to him was Rear Admiral Halil Pasha, the superintendent of the disembarkation of stores at the Port of Haifa. Despite their inexperience in railroad management, Cevad Pasha and 50 other military officers of various ranks were assigned to help the administration in Haifa[6].

The factory and repair centers required an enclosed area of 8,000 square meters. Including the cost of machinery, their establishment cost approximately 1,000,000 francs[7]. After the completion of the Hejaz Railway, it was assumed that the goods office would be moved to Damascus, the capital of Syria, in part because the provincial authorities resided there and because communication proved very difficult. Doing so would further facilitate the communication between the Beirut-Damascus-Aleppo line's administration and the commercial companies located in Damascus.

It was eventually decided that Damascus would hold the headquarters of the line administration and Qadem al-Sharif, the location of the Damascus Station and the main repair center. A big terminal with offices was built in the main square near the new Government Serai, or Palace, overlooking the Barada Valley. The Qadem Station was retained and the line continued all the way to the terminus passing close to the Maidan and Beramke stations of the French line. As a result, Damascus became the center of administration, construction, and maintenance[8].

---

5   L/P&S/10/12, "From Sir N. O'Conor to Sir Edward Grey (Confidential)," Istanbul, 12 June 1906 in *IOR*.

6   L/P&S/10/12, "From Mr. G. Barclay to Sir Edward Grey (Confidential)," Istanbul, 17 November 1906 in *IOR*.

7   L/P&S/10/12, "From Mr. G. Barclay to Sir Edward Grey (Confidential)," Istanbul, 17 November 1906 in *IOR*.

8   L/P&S/10/12, "From Mr. G. Barclay to Sir Edward Grey (Confidential)," Istanbul, 17 November 1906 in *IOR*.

A 150-room hotel replaced the Old Serai, made of fine stone, which became a major tourist attraction. Most of the workshops and repair centers were erected to the east of the Qadem Station. Ordered from Baume and Marpent, Haino St. Pierre, Belgium, the machinery ran on electrical power provided by the power station of the Tramway Company, a Belgian concession, located in suburban Ain al-Fijé, which supplied electricity to the town and tramways, as well. This arrangement established the principal construction and repair site for the line. In addition, smaller repair centers were to be constructed in Deraa, Al-Ula, Ma'an, Medina, Tabuk and Haifa.

Al-Ula and Tabuk were selected on account of their rich water supplies and a new terminal, hotel, and repair center brought their own advantages. The permanent base was well built and the bridges were solidly constructed. The active Traffic Department of the sections was less than satisfactory, thereby causing vast confusion and a need to reform the existing system[9].

New Commissions Established to Administer the Construction

The General Commission for the construction of the Hejaz Railway was established in Istanbul[10]. As its president, the Grand Vizier led the members selected from influential and respected officials such as İzzet Pasha, the Minister of Public Works and the Director of the Factories of the Imperial Marine Arsenal. In addition, some officials were appointed as technical advisors from the Ministry of Public Works. In coordination with the High Commission in Istanbul, smaller commissions were formed in certain cities[11].

Damascus also hosted the Local Commission for the construction of the Hejaz Railroad, which decided the operation schemes[12]. The President of the

---

9   L/P&S/10/12, "From Mr. G. Barclay to Sir Edward Grey (Confidential)," Istanbul, 17 November 1906 in *IOR*.

10   L/P&S/10/12, "From Mr. G. Barclay to Sir Edward Grey (Confidential)," Istanbul, 17 November 1906 in *IOR*; L/P&S/10/12, "From Sir N. O'Conor to Sir Edward Grey (Confidential)," Istanbul, 12 June 1906 in *IOR*.

11   L/P&S/10/12, "From Mr. G. Barclay to Sir Edward Grey (Confidential)," Istanbul, 17 November 1906 in *IOR*.

12   FO 78/5452, "H.R. O'Conor," Istanbul 23 May 1900; L/P&S/10/12, "From Mr. G. Barclay to Sir Edward Grey (Confidential)," Istanbul, 17 November 1906 in *IOR*; and L/P&S/10/12, "From Sir N. O'Conor to Sir Edward Grey (Confidential)," Istanbul, 12 June 1906 in *IOR*.

commission was the Governor of Damascus and the members were the Commander-General of the 5th Army and Kazım Pasha[13], the Director-General of the Hejaz Railway, and a local notable as well. The technical division of the commission included the chief engineer, Heinrich August Meissner Pasha[14] of German origin, who was appointed as the new Director of the Engineering Works of the Railroad's Construction[15], in January 1901, and several Turkish engineers who specialized in railroad construction[16].

The President of the Local Commission was the Governor of Damascus. In practice, Müşir (the Field-Marshal) Kazım Pasha acted as the Chief of the Construction Department and Meissner Pasha, who already gained the confidence and respect of the Commission back in Istanbul, was the main driving-force behind the entire project. Meissner Pasha built a house in Ma'an and worked with M. Schroder, his principal assistant from France, at the construction offices there[17].

The official task of the Local Commission was to examine the proposals and plans of the Director-General and forward them to the Istanbul Commission to be processed. The commission was responsible for seeking out and applying for the construction's funding, land acquisitions, appointing engineers and officials, and making contracts for supplies and tools[18]. The fact that a certain portion of the railroad was completed quickly illustrates that high circles grasped the significance and extent of the project[19]. In fact, the Board of Management and Works achieved its desired goals for the project[20], as shall be seen in the following pages.

---

13   L/P&S/10/12, "From Mr. G. Barclay to Sir Edward Grey (Confidential)," Istanbul, 17 November 1906 in *IOR*.

14   L/P&S/10/12, "From Mr. G. Barclay to Sir Edward Grey (Confidential)," Istanbul, 17 November 1906 in *IOR*.

15   L/P&S/10/12, "From Sir N. O'Conor to Sir Edward Grey (Confidential)," Istanbul, 12 June 1906 in *IOR*.

16   L/P&S/10/12, "From Mr. G. Barclay to Sir Edward Grey (Confidential)," Istanbul, 17 November 1906 in *IOR*.

17   L/P&S/10/12, "From Mr. G. Barclay to Sir Edward Grey (Confidential)," Istanbul, 17 November 1906 in *IOR*.

18   L/P&S/10/12, "From Mr. G. Barclay to Sir Edward Grey (Confidential)," Istanbul, 17 November 1906 in *IOR*.

19   L/P&S/10/12, "W.S. Richards," Damascus, 8 February 1902 in *IOR*.

20   L/P&S/10/12, "From Sir N. O'Conor to Sir Edward Grey (Confidential)," Istanbul, 12 June 1906 in *IOR*.

SURVEYING THE HEJAZ RAILWAY

An imperial edict issued by the Sultan ordered surveying of the first part of the Hejaz Railway, tracing the lines, charting estimated costs, and presenting comprehensive reports to the High Commission[21].

Under Hacı Muhtar Bey, the technical advisor to the Hejaz Railway, Turkish engineers surveyed the Damascus-Muzeirib-Deraa section. It did not take long for the Ottoman government to realize that the ignorance and disorganization of Turkish engineers slowed the progress of the project. Whereas the Ottoman government wanted the Hejaz Railway to be an Ottoman product from planning to completion, it had no choice but to appoint a famous and distinguished German engineer, Meissner, as the Chief Engineer and Director of Construction[22] on a three-year provisional contract, starting in January 1901[23]. Meissner began by forming multiethnic surveying crews, including European and Ottoman engineers, and then naming the railway, "Le Chemin de Fer Hamidieh du Hejaz"[24].

Another distinguished engineer, Privy Councilor of the German Emperor and Inspector of the Hama-Aleppo Railroad for six years and the previous surveyor of the main line to Mecca, Otto von Kapp Kohlstein, revealed the real potential of Muhtar Bey, who worked under his supervision. Muhtar Bey proved to Kohlstein that he was an efficient and knowledgeable inspector[25]. Muhtar Bey later joined a pilgrim caravan from Damascus to Mecca, observing and measuring the line[26]. Muhtar Bey completed the survey of the

---

21 L/P&S/10/12, "From Sir N. O'Conor to Sir Edward Grey (Confidential)," Istanbul, 12 June 1906 in *IOR*.
22 L/P&S/10/12, "From U.F.S. to Foreign Office," Therapia, 6 August 1906 in *IOR*; L/P&S/10/12, "From Mr. G. Barclay to Sir Edward Grey (Confidential)," Istanbul, 17 November 1906 in *IOR*.
23 L/P&S/10/12, "From U.F.S. to Foreign Office," Therapia, 6 August 1906 in *IOR*; L/P&S/10/12, "From Mr. G. Barclay to Sir Edward Grey (Confidential)," Istanbul, 17 November 1906 in *IOR*.
24 L/P&S/10/12, "From Sir N. O'Conor to Sir Edward Grey (Confidential)," Istanbul, 12 June 1906 in *IOR*.
25 L/P&S/10/12, "From Sir N. O'Conor to Sir Edward Grey (Confidential)," Istanbul, 12 June 1906 in *IOR*.
26 L/P&S/10/12, "From Mr. G. Barclay to Sir Edward Grey (Confidential)," Istanbul, 17 November 1906 in *IOR*.

line in Medina and, eventually, continued until Medain Saleh[27]. Muhtar reported the survey results with a map under a sectional profile.

A daunting challenge of this project was the fact that there were not enough stations along the telegraph lines to facilitate the inspection. For instance, the stations on the main line between Ma'an and Medina, a distance of 700 kilometers, were too few to conduct a proper inspection[28].

In line with the imperial edict issued in 1901, the High Commission in Istanbul took effective measures. Due to the concerted efforts of the Damascus Commission, Kazım Pasha, the Minister of Construction and the Director-General of the Hejaz Railway[29] and of its construction[30], and Meissner, the construction plan developed significantly. Particularly, the Local Commission's enthusiasm and the dedication of Nazım Pasha, its president and the local governor, gave the construction speed, efficiency, and promise. The fine-tuned coordination between the civil engineers and the commanders of the Ottoman imperial troops who worked during the construction, point to the administrative skills of Kazım Pasha[31] and the fact that all parties involved were very devoted to the project.

TRACKS, MACHINES, AND WAGONS: GENERAL CHARACTERISTICS

PLAN OF CONSTRUCTION

The main line of the Hejaz Railway ran parallel to the Syrian and Arabian coasts. In particular, the line ran from Damascus to Ma'an on a 20-degree parallel with the Syrian coast, Ma'an to Medina was completely parallel to the coast, Medina to Mecca curved towards the southwest and took a southeastern direction to Mecca between Messtura and Kachima, as it approached the Red Sea.

---

[27] L/P&S/10/12, "From U.F.S. to Foreign Office," Therapia, 6 August 1906 in *IOR*.

[28] L/P&S/10/12, "From Mr. G. Barclay to Sir Edward Grey (Confidential)," Istanbul, 17 November 1906 in *IOR*.

[29] L/P&S/10/12, "From Sir N. O'Conor to Sir Edward Grey (Confidential)," Istanbul, 12 June 1906 in *IOR*.

[30] FO 195/2286, "J.H. McMohan," Jeddah, 23 April 1908.

[31] L/P&S/10/12, "From Sir N. O'Conor to Sir Edward Grey (Confidential)," Istanbul, 12 June 1906 in *IOR*.

The distance between stations connecting Damascus and Deraa was 14 kilometers and 24 kilometers between Deraa and Mudawarra. The scarcity of water between Deraa and Mudawwara was very challenging for travelers[32].

RAILWAY ROUTE/S

The sectional profile of the railway line followed the historical, pilgrimage-caravan road. The line resided to the east of the road between Damascus and Zerqa and similarly up to Mudawwara, occasionally changing sides of the road to avoid hills and rough ground[33].

A 340-meter rise in height from Zerqa to the plateau in southern Amman required the line's first divergence from the original pilgrimage route. A series of curves extended over three kilometers with steep gradients of up to 20/1,000, with a 100-meter radius. Therefore, this section of the line required intense, hard work. For instance, 20-meter-high, 12-meter-wide viaducts had to be built from hewn-stones and a 140-meter long tunnel, the only tunnel on the main line, had to be built[34].

A 150-meter rise in height between Ma'an and Batn al-Ghul did not require the same work. Instead, there was a series of curves extending over eight kilometers, with a gradient of 18/1,000 and with a 100-meter radius. After these two spots, the rail line passed through only a few valleys that were covered by 3 to 60-meter long bridges. Since the bedrock was not far below the surface, it served as a good foundation and the risk of flooding was very low. As a result, a gradient of 18/1,000 sufficed on straight sections. The curved sections had an even smaller gradient[35]. The straight pilgrimage route had to be redirected near Batn al-Ghul because the clay-bed could cause the embankment to shift. In addition, sand drifts that were two-meters deep had to be avoided near Mudawwara[36].

---

32 L/P&S/10/12, "From Sir N. O'Conor to Sir Edward Grey (Confidential)," Istanbul, 12 June 1906 in *IOR*, p. 484.

33 L/P&S/10/12, "From Mr. G. Barclay to Sir Edward Grey (Confidential)," Istanbul, 17 November 1906 in *IOR*.

34 L/P&S/10/12, "From Mr. G. Barclay to Sir Edward Grey (Confidential)," Istanbul, 17 November 1906 in *IOR*.

35 Ibid; and L/P&S/10/12, "From Sir N. O'Conor to Sir Edward Grey (Confidential)," Istanbul, 12 June 1906 in *IOR*.

36 L/P&S/10/12, "From Mr. G. Barclay to Sir Edward Grey (Confidential)," Istanbul, 17 November 1906 in *IOR*.

There were no settlements in Muzeirib, Deraa, Nessib, Mafraq, Khir-bet al-Samra, Zerqa, or Amman. While the Zerqa station on the main line was quite far from the village of the same name, there was a decent sized village close to the line in Amman and a small township neighbored the line in Deraa [37].

BEDDING THE TRACKS

The bedding consisted of a solid mixture of lava, basalt, and flint-rubble. Wooden grids were laid up to Zerqa and iron sleepers attached the rails from there. The stones needed for the bedding were abundant along the route. Better yet, the size of the stones was suitable to break into small pieces. However, it was soon discovered that that the wooden sleepers were not suitable for desert climate: the wood shrank under the heat and then split. As a result, the nails loosened and failed to hold the rails in their vertical position. A change in the gauge was crucial as the wagons oscillated when they passed over the lines. It was from then on that only iron sleepers were used[38].

GAUGING THE TRACKS

The Hejaz Railroad was a narrow railroad with a 1.05-meter wide gauge. Its narrow size was due to the fact that the project was only possible with the contributions of the Muslim community, who were already suffering from economic stagnation. Also, a narrow gauge line, according to the

---

[37] L/P&S/10/12, "From Mr. G. Barclay to Sir Edward Grey (Confidential)," Istanbul, 17 November 1906 in *IOR*.

L/P&S/10/12, "From Mr. G. Barclay to Sir Edward Grey (Confidential)," Istanbul, 17 November 1906 in *IOR*.

L/P&S/10/12, "From Mr. G. Barclay to Sir Edward Grey (Confidential)," Istanbul, 17 November 1906 in *IOR*.

L/P&S/10/12, "From Mr. G. Barclay to Sir Edward Grey (Confidential)," Istanbul, 17 November 1906 in *IOR*.

L/P&S/10/12, "From Mr. G. Barclay to Sir Edward Grey (Confidential)," Istanbul, 17 November 1906 in *IOR*.

L/P&S/10/12, "From Sir N. O'Conor to Sir Edward Grey (Confidential)," Istanbul, 12 JuneFO 78/5452, "From Consul W. S. Richards to Sir N. O'Conor," Damascus, 4 November 1902.

[38] L/P&S/10/12, "From Mr. G. Barclay to Sir Edward Grey (Confidential)," Istanbul, 17 November 1906 in *IOR*.

opinions of the engineers', was much easier to build than a broader one. The Beirut-Damascus line, the only connection between the Hejaz Railway and the sea after the construction of the Haifa-Deraa line, also had a narrow gauge. Lastly, it was unlikely that the traffic on the prospective road would be congested. While the line between Riyaq and Beirut in Lebanon was narrow, the alternative line between Riyaq and Aleppo had the only broad-gauge line in that section[39].

WEIGHING THE TRACKS

The rails weighed 21.5 kilograms per meter, while the railroad, including rails, sleepers, and appurtenances, totaled up to 103 kilograms[40].

PAVING FOR THE RAILWAY

The groundwork of the railroad required a great deal of masonry. The tunnel and large viaduct near Amman were the most substantial works built. In the Damascus-Mudawwara section, there were 462 bridges, 271 aqueducts, and 799 culverts, a total of 1,532 engineering works including the viaduct. While a 15-meter long bridge was iron, all other works were made of stone. Some culverts had arches and the others were cemented under the rails. Despite the adverse effects of the suffocating heat and dryness on the labor force, the masonry involved in the construction was successful.

The lime and sandstone, which was readily available along most of the route, provided an excellent source of building material. In the construction of the heavy bridges, one or more arches were built ranging from 3 to 12 meters in width. The openings of the culverts varied from 0.40 to 2 meters, depending on yearly rainfall estimates. In one instance, the Director of Railroad Construction witnessed an unexpected amount of rainfall in, otherwise, dry valleys in the region, in the winter of 1904-1905. That particular season, the highlands in eastern Jordan, especially those beyond Amman, recorded an all-time high of rainfall. The railroad crossed a valley to the south of the

---

39 L/P&S/10/12, "From Mr. G. Barclay to Sir Edward Grey (Confidential)," Istanbul, 17 November 1906 in *IOR*.

40 L/P&S/10/12, "From Mr. G. Barclay to Sir Edward Grey (Confidential)," Istanbul, 17 November 1906 in *IOR*.

Kassir Station with the help of a dike and the rainfall estimates required the building of the following[41]:

A three-meter wide bridge with six arches, a three-meter wide bridge with four arches, a three-meter wide bridge with three arches and a three-meter wide bridge with two arches.

However, these were not sufficient. As a result, the standing water was unable to pour out and caused the collapse of the bridge, with its 20-meter dikes. Under pouring rain, a train with five open and closed wagons running 20 km/h approached the collapsed section and the driver of the train failed to notice it until the train was five meters from it. Too late to break or back up, the train fell into the collapsed section, but the five passenger wagons stopping safely on the dike. Fortunately, there were no casualties or major injuries. The damage to the stock was minor and the Kraus locomotive suffered hardly any damage. Excluding the dike damaged in this incident, the heavy rains in the winter of 1904-1905 inflicted no damage on the main line, and in its first season of operation, the Hejaz Railway passed this test[42].

CONSTRUCTING THE RAILWAY

Gauge	: 1 meter
Rails	: Vignola's system: 8 meters in length, 20 kilograms in weight
Sleepers	: Made of wood and steel
Tunnels	: A single tunnel between Zerqa and Kassir
Curves	: 100-meter radius minimum
Gradients	: 20/100 maximum

While each kilogram of rail cost 50,000 francs, including the rolling stock, the cost doubled in the Haifa branch to 100,000 francs[43].

---

[41] L/P&S/10/12, "From Mr. G. Barclay to Sir Edward Grey (Confidential)," Istanbul, 17 November 1906 in *IOR*.

[42] L/P&S/10/12, "From Mr. G. Barclay to Sir Edward Grey (Confidential)," Istanbul, 17 November 1906 in *IOR*.

[43] L/P&S/10/12, "From Sir N. O'Conor to Sir Edward Grey (Confidential)," Istanbul, 12 June 1906 in *IOR*.

SERVICING THE RAILWAY

Engines   : 26-10 of 70 tons, 10 of 40 tons, and
                   approximately 200 wagons

Running speeds : 30 km/h average[44]

ROLLING STOCK

Engines

High gradients in the Yarmuk Valley and in southern Amman required the Hejaz Railway to purchase high-power, duplex engines to grapple with the traffic jams in these areas. Eight engines were purchased and shipped from Henschel and Sohn of Cassel. Six of them operated in the Yarmuk section however, they weighed nearly 60 tons. Since the engines were too heavy to run on the existing light rails, they were derailed a number of times. The rails varied from 38 to 42 lbs. per yard and only the Haifa Branch had rails of 52 lbs. per yard[45].

Locomotives

There were 12 Kraus locomotives with three axles, each weighing 30 tons with a capacity of 3.5 cubic meters and nine locomotives with four axles, each weighing 40 tons with a capacity of 12.5 cubic meters. Four "B" Hohenzollern locomotives with a small engine capacity served the Haifa branch. In total, 33 engines were in use and received regular maintenance. There were 12 other engines, but they were not maintained for normal operation and were only used for shunting purposes, instead of running in regular traffic[46]. This being the case, the commission ordered six passenger locomotives at a speed of 45 kilometers and thirteen 13 merchandise trains. In total, the Hejaz Railway operated 43 locomotives — 39 were up-to-date — and 400 wagons, including 135 wagons that had been ordered[47].

---

44 L/P&S/10/12, "From Sir N. O'Conor to Sir Edward Grey (Confidential)," Istanbul, 12 June 1906 in *IOR*.

45 L/P&S/10/12, "From Mr. G. Barclay to Sir Edward Grey (Confidential)," Istanbul, 17 November 1906 in *IOR*.

46 L/P&S/10/12, "From Mr. G. Barclay to Sir Edward Grey (Confidential)," Istanbul, 17 November 1906 in *IOR*.

47 L/P&S/10/12, "From Sir N. O'Conor to Sir Edward Grey (Confidential)," Istanbul, 12 June 1906 in *IOR*.

Wagons

There were several double-axle wagons weighing 7.5 tons and able to carry 15 tons, 15 third-class passenger-cars, a first-class passenger car, and a mosque-wagon built at the Admiralty workshops[48]. Miscellaneous rolling stock was as follows:

5 sleeping saloons to serve high officials and select tourists

2 first-class carriages working in Haifa during the high season and on special occasions

19 third-class carriages

100 covered wagons

145 open-platform wagons

6 custom-made wagons to carry livestock[49].

Saechs Maschinen Fabrik of Richard Hartmann in Chemnitz (established in 1906) and Arn. Jung, Jungenthal bei Kirchen in Rheinland (established in 1900), two German firms, built the Kraus engines. Belgian firms built the carriages and wagons and garnered several important machinery contracts. Two main Belgian firms involved were Société Anonymo Belge, Lion Hiard, Directeur and Usines et Fonderies de Baume et Marpent, Usine de Morlanweiss, Haine St. Pierre, Belgique, the latter obtaining the majority of the contracts. Several other firms supplied the rails. The final contract was given to a French-Belgian firm based in Russia, which marked its rails with "Providence-Russe, 1906". As for the quality of their work, there were complaints that the iron used was of very soft quality and prone to bend. In addition, Cockerill, a large Belgian firm, the American Steel Trust — its rails were marked with "Maryland, VII-IIIIIII"— and a German firm in Donawitz had the other contracts[50].

While some of the aforementioned wagons were partially covered, the rest were entirely open. Most of the freight consisted of railroad stuffs and grain in the first eight years therefore, it required purchasing several wagons with a capacity of 30 tons. In fact, the wagons had to weigh nine tons if the axles were to hold up to 60 tons so that they could run under 30 tons. The

---

[48] L/P&S/10/12, "From Sir N. O'Conor to Sir Edward Grey (Confidential)," Istanbul, 12 June 1906 in *IOR*.

[49] L/P&S/10/12, "From Mr. G. Barclay to Sir Edward Grey (Confidential)," Istanbul, 17 November 1906 in *IOR*.

[50] L/P&S/10/12, "From Mr. G. Barclay to Sir Edward Grey (Confidential)," Istanbul, 17 November 1906 in *IOR*.

cost of these wagons was cheaper compared to others and the maintenance costs were equal to the 15-ton wagons. The first order of wagons was not equipped with the same coupling system as those on the Beirut-Damascus-Hanran line. However, this problem was resolved by ordering a new set of wagons that replaced the older ones on a regular basis[51].

The covered wagons were ideal for carrying troops, mainly because they provided protection from the sun and cold winds of winter. The peasants on the trains started a habit of lying on the floor. The interior floor space was 27 feet by 6 feet 10 inches, had double-sliding doors on each side with either a 4 foot or an 8 foot-wide opening. The sides of the open-platform wagons were designed to descend. Although this type of wagon had no shelter, they were generally used to carry troops, pilgrims, and workmen. Their interior floor space was 31 feet by 7 feet, 10 inches, and could carry 40 to 45 passengers.

Each 15-ton covered wagon could carry six to eight small, Syrian ponies. The tare weight of a covered wagon was 8.5 tons. The length of military trains was regulated according to the weight that the engines could haul up the steep gradients of the Yarmuk Valley and Amman. For example, a typical engine could haul six trucks, each loaded with 10 tons of goods. With 40 people in each and the loaded goods put together, the numbers could reach 240 people for each truck, or 60 tons of goods. This was the maximum an engine could run with on the long, Yarmuk Valley incline. In Amman, it was possible to take the train up in two sections of five carriages each. The new duplex locomotives were able to carry double the mentioned weights, but they would then be too heavy for the rails to bear[52].

BRAKES, COUPLINGS, AND SIGNALING

All the carriages that were initially equipped with hand brakes began to gradually use Hardy's system of automatic brakes, which was already compatible for some engines and carriages at the Haifa branch. A safer coupling method replaced the single buffer and hook, which was likely to break easily. The use of double-screw couplings and double chains solved the problem. The signaling was very simple; the train driver received a pa-

---

51 L/P&S/10/12, "From Sir N. O'Conor to Sir Edward Grey (Confidential)," Istanbul, 12 June 1906 in *IOR*.

52 L/P&S/10/12, "From Mr. G. Barclay to Sir Edward Grey (Confidential)," Istanbul, 17 November 1906 in *IOR*.

per message from the stationmaster that read "clear line", directing the train to the next stop. Except for the green and white lights used at night, there were no other signals[53].

CONDITION OF THE ROLLING STOCK

The existing rolling stock of the Hejaz Railway suffered from a lack of maintenance. Third-class carriages, the only passenger vehicles, did not usually have glasses in the windows and the roof leaked when it rained. Over-heated axles were not an uncommon problem. In one instance, the wooden beams of a wagon with a 25-ton load collapsed and it was left behind at a wayside station. The travelling pilgrims complained a lot about the windowless carriages and open-platform wagons that they were forced to travel aboard. Therefore, many pilgrims continued to travel by road, as was tradition, while some left the Hejaz line in Deraa, crossed over to Muzeirib, and took the French line to Damascus. The mosque-carriage, a specially designed construction by the arsenal in Istanbul, remained unused and discarded in a siding[54] in Deraa. Since the woodwork was unseasoned, the wooden structure often warped and split, the curtains ripped, and the floor was a mess. In addition, the ventilation system functioned poorly and the carriages, too wide for the gauge, presented great dangers when excessive rolling occurred in motion. The average traveler did not enjoy sleeping in the saloon carriages reserved for high officials and rich tourists, who were willing to pay extra for the service[55].

British officials thought that a European traffic manager could skillfully manipulate Rıza Pasha so that the Turks would fix all these shortcomings, which in turn would increase the incoming profit from the Hejaz Railway. The existing situation was not promising and they believed that this was the only way to ameliorate the railway. The replacement of M. Gaudin with a British official was also desired strongly for it would raise the service quality to British standards and get the system to work[56].

---

[53] L/P&S/10/12, "From Mr. G. Barclay to Sir Edward Grey (Confidential)," Istanbul, 17 November 1906 in *IOR*.

[54] A siding is a secondary railroad track connected to the main track. Wooden strips or similar materials were used to cover the sides of buildings.

[55] L/P&S/10/12, "From Mr. G. Barclay to Sir Edward Grey (Confidential)," Istanbul, 17 November 1906 in *IOR*.

[56] L/P&S/10/12, "From Mr. G. Barclay to Sir Edward Grey (Confidential)," Istanbul, 17 November 1906 in *IOR*.

PART TWO

Daunting Challenges to the Railway Construction

DAUNTING CHALLENGES TO THE
RAILWAY CONSTRUCTION

SHORTCOMINGS OF THE RAILWAY CONSTRUCTION

The Hejaz Railway faced problems with construction, finance, and diplomacy, the three major shortcomings that had to be solved. Diplomatic problems complicated determining the railway route, accommodating possible public prejudice, and maintaining the balance of local commerce.

OVERWHELMING PROBLEMS

Water Shortage

From the beginning, water scarcity challenged the construction of the Hejaz Railway, which passed through barren and desert areas. As a matter of fact, water supplies occupied the main agenda of the Hejaz Railway and could only be provided at long intervals[57]. Muhtar Bey reported that the Hejaz Railway would not be subject to significant obstacles in terms of construction. However, the further away the line moved from Damascus and Haifa the more difficult the construction got. Likewise, the water scarcity posed a great threat unless wells were sunk and springs discovered, as was the case in northern Ma'an[58].

The construction went well until Ma'an. A great supply of water was discovered in Petra. The Roalla Bedouins, a large clan from the Aniza tribe, were already using the rich pastures and wells in Al-Udian. Muazzam, the

---

[57] L/P&S/10/12, "From Mr. G. Barclay to Sir Edward Grey (Confidential)," Istanbul, 17 November 1906 in *IOR*.

[58] L/P&S/10/12, "From Sir N. O'Conor to Sir Edward Grey (Confidential)," Istanbul, 12 June 1906 in *IOR*.

nearest spot to Hail, was another plentiful source of water. While some stations were provided with cisterns, others were supplied with springs or wells[59]. The following stations had springs:

Head of the Line, Damascus:

Kilometer (Km) 12, Deraa

Km 203, Zerqa

Km 222, Amman

Km 378, Al-Hassa

Km 458, Ma'an

Km 572, Mudawwara[60]

As in Ma'an, a large water cistern was built in Tabuk. In addition, other water cisterns were constructed in Medina and Al-'Ula, a small nearby town to the south of Medain Saleh with a significant supply of water. Walled and protected, these cisterns, some of which dated back to the Roman Empire, stored rainwater in winter and served travelers in the summer, mostly Bedouins with herds that needed water for drinking and cooking. A huge cistern also held a great quantity of water in Qatrana. The water level in the cistern was shallow and the water it contained had a tendency to evaporate quickly in large quantities. However, putting a roof over the top made the cistern a valuable source of water and solved the problems. Before the railroad, when the pilgrims used it more often, the cistern held 30,000 cubic meters[61]. It was a valuable water supply, although smaller than the cistern in Djeizé, which held 70,000 cubic meters[62]. Both cisterns, uncovered under the sun, had a large surface area and little depth. Consequently, the water evaporated under the heat of the sun, leaving the cisterns empty. In fact, exposure to the sun was common in most areas of construction, thus making water a highly desired commodity. There were sufficient reservoirs of well water on the completed parts of the line in Damascus, Deraa, Zerqa,

---

59 L/P&S/10/12, "From Mr. G. Barclay to Sir Edward Grey (Confidential)," Istanbul, 17 November 1906 in *IOR*.

60 L/P&S/10/12, "From Sir N. O'Conor to Sir Edward Grey (Confidential)," Istanbul, 12 June 1906 in *IOR*.

61 L/P&S/10/12, "From Mr. G. Barclay to Sir Edward Grey (Confidential)," Istanbul, 17 November 1906 in *IOR*.

62 Ibid; and L/P&S/10/12, "From Sir N. O'Conor to Sir Edward Grey (Confidential)," Istanbul, 12 June 1906 in *IOR*.

Amman, Al-Hassa, Ma'an, and Mudawwara, but it was uncertain if it could sustain the railway in service. Again, the further into the desert the construction of the line advanced, the more the lack of water was felt[63].

The procurement of locomotives with tenders of 8-12 cubic meters was considered and executed. In line with this idea, special cistern-wagons and tank-cars were ordered for water transportation[64]. Soon after, water was transported from Qatrana to Ma'an by trucks with large double-tanks filled from wells or cisterns. Steam pumps or wind pumps filled the tanks in one try, because the winds on the highlands were very strong. Since hauling the water proved very costly, they decided that more wells should be sunk and covered; deeper cisterns should be built at 30 to 70 kilometer intervals. After Amman, the intervals were greater because the water scarcity was more severe. Initially though, the proposal suggested that springs be used, as in Mismia[65].

Cisterns were built every 50 to 60 kilometers where wells could not be dug[66], and covering the cisterns helped keep the water in reserves. Delays in providing the construction with water supplies resulted mainly from the fact that the involved officials and workers gave priority to the construction, not the facilities[67]. Six or seven-meter deep and covered, new cisterns prevented rapid evaporation and kept germs out. In fact, the water was potable[68]. The old, shallow, and large-area pools that provided water to the nomads' camels were not covered and were, thus, of little use to the railway. The pools in Qatrana, for example, had a capacity of 36,000 cubic meters while those of Djeizé could hold 70,000 cubic meters. Uncovered, the water in the pools evaporated very quickly and remained empty for months. Since it was very expensive to cover them, it was more logical, financially, to establish cisterns every six or

63 L/P&S/10/12, "From Mr. G. Barclay to Sir Edward Grey (Confidential)," Istanbul, 17 November 1906 in *IOR*.

64 L/P&S/10/12, "From Mr. G. Barclay to Sir Edward Grey (Confidential)," Istanbul, 17 November 1906 in *IOR*.

65 L/P&S/10/12, "From Mr. G. Barclay to Sir Edward Grey (Confidential)," Istanbul, 17 November 1906 in *IOR*.

66 L/P&S/10/12, "From Mr. G. Barclay to Sir Edward Grey (Confidential)," Istanbul, 17 November 1906 in *IOR*.

67 L/P&S/10/12, "From Sir N. O'Conor to Sir Edward Grey (Confidential)," Istanbul, 12 June 1906 in *IOR*.

68 L/P&S/10/12, "From Mr. G. Barclay to Sir Edward Grey (Confidential)," Istanbul, 17 November 1906 in *IOR*.

seven kilometers along the line[69]. Moreover, a filtering apparatus began to be used to improve the drinking quality of the water and artesian wells were dug for healthier water in greater quantities. A Belgian firm signed the contract to carry out these projects. The rocky soil near Zerqa did not permit the boring machine to dig deeper than 30 meters. Hollow basins in eastern Tabuk and other areas near Ma'an promised better results. In general, the earth was composed of limestone and sandstone, with lava beds in certain areas. In Ma'an, water found at a working depth and the construction of wells allowed for the establishment of a large water reservoir and presented a solid solution to the water shortage. However, other locations were not as fortunate as Ma'an. If no surface water was found and no wells successfully constructed, then water could only be extracted from deeper levels and in small quantities. Some areas did not have water to depths down to 110 meters[70].

Windmill pumps, an ideal apparatus for the region, were constructed near the wells. Steady winds and, at times, strong dust storms were typical in the desert, especially in Ma'an and Tabuk. One steam pump was in reserve for each windmill pump, but they were hardly ever used. Water was critical, especially at the head of the railroad. Thousands of workers needed vast amounts of water for mixing mortar, drinking, and cooking. Water supplies were sent to the stations and work camps in iron barrels that were galvanized, strong, and custom-made. They could hold 75 liters or 16.5 gallons and were welded at both ends and closed by a metal screw plug. Two iron barrels of this type were loaded onto a camel in order to support work parties that were far away from the railhead. Trains, also, carried the barrels to the stations that lacked daily liquid supplies mainly water. The strong constitution of the barrels, which had no joints since they were welded at each end and leak-proof, made them suitable for the conditions. Without these iron barrels, Meissner Pasha affirmed, the supply of water would have faltered. In fact, the closest wells that could provide sufficient water to the construction site between Mudawwara and Zat al-Hajj were in Ma'an. Although the water discovered in Mudawwara and Tabuk eased matters to an extent, it was still necessary to transport water between stations. Muhtar Bey previ-

---

[69] L/P&S/10/12, "From Sir N. O'Conor to Sir Edward Grey (Confidential)," Istanbul, 12 June 1906 in *IOR*.

[70] L/P&S/10/12, "From Mr. G. Barclay to Sir Edward Grey (Confidential)," Istanbul, 17 November 1906 in *IOR*.

ously surveyed the areas to the south of Tabuk up to Medain Saleh. He was quite interested in and in favor of the region but did not believe that finding water in the vicinity was likely[71].

It took three days to cover 114-152 kilometers by camel to deliver water from the plentiful wells in Ma'an. In particular, the supply of water to the construction zone required quite a number of camels; therefore, the railroad helped supply water to the construction sites: several wagons that had two tanks holding eight cubic meters of water were sent from Ma'an everyday. The challenge to this method of water transportation was the fact that the line had incomplete sections because the rails were laid faster than the bridges across the valleys, leaving gaps in the lines. The problem was overcome by building an auxiliary line that went down, into the valley and then rejoined the main line. By doing so, the water reached its destination along the line at lower costs. Flooding posed a threat to the auxiliary line only when the districts near the valleys received a significant amount of rain. Indeed, the branch line of Haifa-Deraa had more favorable weather conditions than other places on the main line in Haifa, Tel Shahm, Afule, Samakh and Muzeirib. Rich wells, at that time and later, provided water to the Jordan when its tributaries, like the Yarmuk, dried up in the summer[72].

Energy

Energy was just as important as water to run the Hejaz Railway. Located in a region deprived of major resources of fuel, coal, oil, and wood, Syria and Arabia did not hold great amounts of wood or coal-beds. The districts neighboring the Hejaz Railway and Haifa-Deraa branch line had no resources at all, making the situation worse. Since this was the case, importing coal was indispensable in order to keep the engines and stations functioning. Most coal came from the Cardiff line, except for smaller quantities obtained from Turkish mines in Heraklia, near the Black Sea. Turkish coal, in fact, was not of great value for it was smokier and likely to choke the tubes. Therefore, domestic coal was used in small quantities along with coal from Cardiff. Coal reserves in Haifa were extremely limited and not used to the

---

71 L/P&S/10/12, "From Mr. G. Barclay to Sir Edward Grey (Confidential)," Istanbul, 17 November 1906 in *IOR*.

72 L/P&S/10/12, "From Mr. G. Barclay to Sir Edward Grey (Confidential)," Istanbul, 17 November 1906 in *IOR*.

fullest extent. At one point, the Haifa-Damascus branch stopped working for two consecutive days when the awaited steamer did not arrive in Haifa, due to the irresponsibility of the local administration. Operations resumed only when they borrowed coal from a French company and a British steamer anchored in the harbor[73].

The annual coal consumption on the construction line ranged between 20,000-25,000 tons a year. Typically, each steamer anchored at the Port of Haifa was able to deliver 300 tons of coal a day in good weather during the summer[74].

The central coal depots of the Hejaz Railway and its branch line were located in Damascus and Haifa. Coal, as well as laborers, had to be transported where construction demanded it, in one particular instance to Medina, 1,400 kilometers away. The construction process would have been much more difficult if the region's temperature went below zero. In reality, even winter weather was mild enough to heat the station buildings with minimal costs of energy; primarily, coal was only used to cook and bake for the workers on the line.[75]

There were good sources of chalk near the construction sites, but the lack of energy prevented building limekilns there. According to the estimates, importing lime would cost much less than extracting it at the sites that lacked energy. Therefore, for the requirement of lime mortar, hydraulic lime was imported[76]. At the same time, lighting material was also imported.

Foreign companies running the railroads in Turkey had to resolve the heating and lighting problems that posed serious challenges. The railroad's construction and operation turned out to be quite expensive since it required importing fuel, especially in Medina and other regions far from the central depots[77].

73 L/P&S/10/12, "From Mr. G. Barclay to Sir Edward Grey (Confidential)," Istanbul, 17 November 1906 in *IOR*.

74 L/P&S/10/12, "From Mr. G. Barclay to Sir Edward Grey (Confidential)," Istanbul, 17 November 1906 in *IOR*.

75 L/P&S/10/12, "From Mr. G. Barclay to Sir Edward Grey (Confidential)," Istanbul, 17 November 1906 in *IOR*.

76 L/P&S/10/12, "From Mr. G. Barclay to Sir Edward Grey (Confidential)," Istanbul, 17 November 1906 in *IOR*.

77 L/P&S/10/12, "From Mr. G. Barclay to Sir Edward Grey (Confidential)," Istanbul, 17 November 1906 in *IOR*.

The Russian General Annenkow's Trans-Caspian Railway had suffered from a similar shortage of energy in the Karakum Desert during its construction, because there were no sources of petroleum on either side of the Caspian Sea. However, the available naphtha residuum provided excellent fuel for locomotives, station buildings lighting, and kitchens, as well as for the personal use of workers, such as for cooking at the construction camps. The authorities, inspired by the success of this earlier practice, decided to use the large petroleum and naphtha sources near Mosul for the Hejaz Railway. In order to do this, the end of the Baghdad line had to be extended from Bulgurlu to Mosul. After it was completed and the line was merged with the Damascus-Aleppo line, the British authorities considered the usage of the naphtha reserves in Mosul for the Hejaz Railway[78].

Sand Drifts

Up to Mudawwara, the Hejaz Railway was free of sand drifts. The railroad had, indeed, circumvented the only possible area for sand drifts. The ground was chalky, not sandy, and this provided an ideal foundation for railroad construction. Beyond Mudawwara though, there were several beds of drift, threatening the integrity of the railroad, which could cause the interruption of traffic by swallowing the rails. Furthermore, steady winds on the highlands caused the machinery to clog with sand and dust, which required continuous cleaning. Fortunately for the authorities, the natives' perception of the rolling stock was changing[79].

The efforts of General Annenkow in the construction of the Trans-Caspian Railway offered tangible proof that such difficulties could be overcome. Annenkow had strengthened the railroad foundation exposed to sand drifts by claying the sand bank, applying horizontal layers of wattles, or by planting plants with sand-binding roots, especially wild oats or tamarisk. In high-risk areas, Annenkow put up a balustrade covered with shingles that shielded the tracks from the sand. Without trees or bushes in the near vicinity, it was especially hard to counter the effects of sand drifts as successfully as Annenkow's methods. There was a large amount of clay near the Batn al-Ghul

---

78 L/P&S/10/12, "From Mr. G. Barclay to Sir Edward Grey (Confidential)," Istanbul, 17 November 1906 in *IOR*.

79 L/P&S/10/12, "From Mr. G. Barclay to Sir Edward Grey (Confidential)," Istanbul, 17 November 1906 in *IOR*.

Station and the neighborhood was rich in stones of various sizes. Available stone and clay was adequate to firmly bank the sand in the region and a decent stone-made dam was built parallel to the line that could cope with sand drifts. Considering the amount of work necessary, the Hejaz Railway needed more time and labor[80].

Working at the Construction

The plan was to launch the line from Damascus; however, the political circumstances and the failure to buy the French line from Damascus to Muzeirib altered the plan. Instead, efforts were focused on the construction of the Muzeirib-Deraa section and transporting materials, rolling stock, and other essentials of the French Damascus-Muzeirib line were directed there[81]. It was the laying of the railroad telegraph line, some years later from Damascus via al-Salt and Ma'an to Medina that actually marked the beginning of the construction of the Hejaz lines[82].

Some difficulties slowed the pace of work[83] and an analysis of the ongoing work at the head of the line is critical in examining the difficulties encountered while railroading in the desert.

Three chief zones divided the construction site: the well-advanced reconnoitering (preliminary surveying) zone, the environs of the surveying zone, and the construction zone. Their size depended on base conditions, but it averaged 50 to 150 kilometers. Each zone had special divisions[84] named after their zone as the reconnoitering, surveying, and building parties.

Starting from 1 December 1905, the reconnoitering party worked between the Tabuk and Medain Saleh stations and the survey party worked between the Mudawwara and Zat al-Hajj stations. The building party finished the Mudawwara-Zat al-Hajj section in the summer of l906 and moved on to

---

80 L/P&S/10/12, "From Mr. G. Barclay to Sir Edward Grey (Confidential)," Istanbul, 17 November 1906 in *IOR*.

81 L/P&S/10/12, "From Sir N. O'Conor to Sir Edward Grey (Confidential)," Istanbul, 12 June 1906 in *IOR*.

82 L/P&S/10/12, "From Mr. G. Barclay to Sir Edward Grey (Confidential)," Istanbul, 17 November 1906 in *IOR*.

83 L/P&S/10/12, "From Mr. G. Barclay to Sir Edward Grey (Confidential)," Istanbul, 17 November 1906 in *IOR*.

84 L/P&S/10/12, "From Mr. G. Barclay to Sir Edward Grey (Confidential)," Istanbul, 17 November 1906 in *IOR*.

the Zat al-Hajj-Tabuk section, while the surveying party advanced correspondingly[85].

The reconnoitering party was responsible for surveying the ground for the railroad, using compasses, pedometers, and barometers, and to mark the route of the line. As a result of their surveys, which took a few months, a report was filed along with a sketch. A caravan was assembled, with staff and equipment, for the reconnoitering party to carry out the surveying. The expedition worked in the desert; therefore, tents, fuel, provisions, saddle and pack animals for transportation, and a cavalry unit to protect the party against Bedouin mobs were provided to carry out their duties. A caravan of this type included: one railroad engineer as the leader, two civil engineers or engineer officers, one doctor, 10 railroad soldiers as watchmen, 20 cavalry units, and a large number of camels, horses, and mules to transport personnel and provisions[86].

Negotiating with Foreign Companies

Foreign companies that owned the lines posed another problem. During construction, negotiations were completed with English and French companies (the names of these two companies are not specified in the source material).

The most important negotiations that the General Commission in Istanbul signed were with the French Company for the Beirut-Damascus-Muzeirib lines and the English Company for the Haifa-Damascus line[87].

Negotiations between the General Commission and the French Company

Obtaining the ownership of the Damascus-Muzeirib line was essential to start the railroad directly from Muzeirib, not Damascus, which would save the Hejaz Railroad from laying down an additional 120 kilometers of rail. However, the effort was not successful. Negotiations between the General Commission and the French Company came to no avail since the company did not accept a generous offer of 7,000,000 francs. With the failure of the

---

[85] L/P&S/10/12, "From Mr. G. Barclay to Sir Edward Grey (Confidential)," Istanbul, 17 November 1906 in *IOR*.

[86] L/P&S/10/12, "From Mr. G. Barclay to Sir Edward Grey (Confidential)," Istanbul, 17 November 1906 in *IOR*.

[87] L/P&S/10/12, "From Mr. G. Barclay to Sir Edward Grey (Confidential)," Istanbul, 17 November 1906 in *IOR*.

negotiations, the General Commission decided to build a Damascus-Deraa line, parallel to the French Damascus-Muzeirib line. Negotiations resumed, but they did not yield any further results and interrupted the work between Damascus-Deraa for a whole year[88].

Although it was mainly due to the reluctance of the French Railroad Company that interrupted the work by withholding the negotiations, the delay in delivering sleepers and rails also contributed to the interruption[89].

The eventual failure of the negotiations encouraged the idea of shifting the new line to Deraa off Muzeirib[90]. This section of the line was opened in September 1905[91].

The French Company refused to let the materials needed for the construction pass along their Beirut-Muzeirib line at a decent rate. To deal with this issue, the Ottoman Government sped up the construction of the Deraa-Haifa branch of the line in an effort to deliver the materials via that route.[92] The French company lost profit after the opening of the Damascus-Haifa line, because commercial activity and traffic were then shifted to Haifa[93].

The Damascus-Deraa section of the Hejaz line did not pass through Muzeirib; instead, an extension connected Muzeirib to Deraa. That became the case based on the assumption that the Ottoman government would buy the existing French line once the construction of the Hejaz line started.

Negotiations between the General Commission and the English Company

Compared to the French Company, negotiations with the English Company were far more successful, because the latter was in financial straits and the

---

88 L/P&S/10/12, "From Mr. G. Barclay to Sir Edward Grey (Confidential)," Istanbul, 17 November 1906 in *IOR*.

89 L/P&S/10/12, "From Mr. G. Barclay to Sir Edward Grey (Confidential)," Istanbul, 17 November 1906 in *IOR*.

90 FO 78/5452, "From Sir Consul W. S. Richards to Sir N. O'Conor," Damascus, 4 November 1902.

91 L/P&S/10/12, "From Mr. G. Barclay to Sir Edward Grey (Confidential)," Istanbul, 17 November 1906 in *IOR*.

92 FO 78/5452, "From Sir Consul W. S. Richards to Sir N. O'Conor," Damascus, 15 December 1903.

93 L/P&S/10/12, "From Mr. G. Barclay to Sir Edward Grey (Confidential)," Istanbul, 17 November 1906 in *IOR*.

entire line had an eight-kilometer sub-structure from Haifa to Reisan. The Commission paid the company 925,000 German marks and bought the concession. Besides the negotiations with the French and British companies, land acquisitions from other sources were relatively easy.

Engineering

As the first Turkish-majority enterprise in railroads, the Hejaz Railway desperately needed ardor and more experience. The Imperial Engineering School, the Ottoman school that educated civil engineers, was only 22 years old and its graduates did not have field training, because there were no government railroads. Later, the General Commission for the construction of the Hejaz Railway was founded in Istanbul. However, it relied on foreign assistance even more than the construction itself and the commission contracted a group of foreign engineers. This fact was evident in the upper level positions in the management of traffic, workshops, and others: French, Austrian, and, especially, German engineers contracted from foreign firms held top positions in the enterprise. The well thought-out and financially sound recruitment process of first class engineers is proof of the Ottoman government's determination and devotion to the Hejaz Railway Project. In 1906, records indicate that there were 10 foreign and 25 Turkish engineers involved in the railroad work, in addition to the engineer officers. For instance, after German Meissner Pasha earned the trust of the Commission in Istanbul, he was appointed Chief Engineer. M. Schroder from France became his principal assistant[94].

Meissner Pasha, as the Chief Engineer, was also responsible for the technical management of the construction, so he assumed both the titles of Chief Engineer and Director of the Engineering Works of the Railroad Construction. His appointment was wise in retrospect.[95]. In fact, Meissner was well-suited for the job: he had previously worked with Otto von Kapp Kohlstein[96] and served in many railroad projects in European Turkey for many years.

---

[94] L/P&S/10/12, "From Mr. G. Barclay to Sir Edward Grey (Confidential)," Istanbul, 17 November 1906 in *IOR*.

[95] L/P&S/10/12, "From Mr. G. Barclay to Sir Edward Grey (Confidential)," Istanbul, 17 November 1906 in *IOR*.

[96] L/P&S/10/12, "From Sir N. O'Conor to Sir Edward Grey (Confidential)," Istanbul, 12 June 1906 in *IOR*.

Otto von Kapp Kohlstein laid over 1,800 kilometers of railroad in the Ottoman Empire. The figures are below:

Name	Length (km)	Construction Duration (in years)	Annual average (in km)
Izmit-Ankara	486	4	121
Salonica-Bitola	220	3	73
Salonica-Alexandroupoli	510	3	170
Alaşehir-Afyon	252	2½	100
Riyaq-Aleppo	332	2½	133
Total	1,800	15	120

The construction of the first four lines listed above began in January 1899 and finished in 12 years, with an average of 144 kilometers laid per year. His experience in these projects gave Otto von Kapp Kohlstein the idea that the Hejaz Railway would become the crowning achievement of all railroading enterprises in the Ottoman Empire[97]. His experience in the field gave him tremendous motivation and confidence that was evident in his finished work, the Hejaz Railway. Meissner, as well, worked on the new project, but his nonstop schedule exhausted him, forcing him to take a vacation and rest[98].

Along with Otto von Kapp Kohlstein's team, there were several other engineers: some distinguished civil engineers, who were graduates of the Imperial Engineering School, were recruited to assistant engineering positions and some as sectional chiefs. Kohlstein believed that they would become first-rate engineers after they acquired practical knowledge in the field[99]. During construction, a number of engineering students became competent engineers, meeting the requests and expectations they were entrusted with[100].

---

97 L/P&S/10/12, "From Sir N. O'Conor to Sir Edward Grey (Confidential)," Istanbul, 12 June 1906 in *IOR*.

98 L/P&S/10/12, "From Sir N. O'Conor to Sir Edward Grey (Confidential)," Istanbul, 12 June 1906 in *IOR*.

99 L/P&S/10/12, "From Sir N. O'Conor to Sir Edward Grey (Confidential)," Istanbul, 12 June 1906 in *IOR*.

100 L/P&S/10/12, "From Mr. G. Barclay to Sir Edward Grey (Confidential)," Istanbul, 17 November 1906 in *IOR*.

Importing Essential Equipments

Without domestic factories, the Hejaz Railway had to import essential materials. Mainly the rails and rolling stock came from abroad: American, Belgian, and German companies supplied rails and sleepers while only Belgian and German companies supplied the rolling stock. Only a minimum number of carriages were produced domestically, at the Ottoman Imperial Marine Arsenal[101].

The cost of importing the material was very high, however an abundance of building material for stone bridges and bedding in the region, except for lime and cement, reduced overall costs. For instance, stones, a very good material for bridges and station buildings, were plentiful along the line and wood beams for roofing were available in Haifa. Iron, unavailable in the region, was not imported at all; as a result there were no iron bridges or other ironworks along the Hejaz Railway[102].

The progress of the construction depended, considerably, on providing food and water supplies to the soldiers, engineers, masons, and workers who were responsible for leveling and building. Supplies had to be transported by the railroad; therefore, a train service was scheduled from Ma'an to deliver their basic needs[103].

Tensions between the Workers

Apparent tensions between the workers of different nationalities slowed the construction of the Hejaz Railway in some respects[104]. The Italian workers at the front line, for instance, in Riyaq, quarreled with the native workers so often that the Governor requested that contractors no longer hire them. When put into force, this meant dismissing a minimum of 1,500 workers. It would be too challenging to fill their gap, since Italians were good workers.

---

[101] L/P&S/10/12, "From Mr. G. Barclay to Sir Edward Grey (Confidential)," Istanbul, 17 November 1906 in *IOR*.

[102] L/P&S/10/12, "From Mr. G. Barclay to Sir Edward Grey (Confidential)," Istanbul, 17 November 1906 in *IOR*.

[103] L/P&S/10/12, "From Sir N. O'Conor to Sir Edward Grey (Confidential)," Istanbul, 12 June 1906 in *IOR*.

[104] L/P&S/10/12, "From Mr. G. Barclay to Sir Edward Grey (Confidential)," Istanbul, 17 November 1906 in *IOR*.

However, there were also other problems mostly ensued from their heavy drinking after work[105].

Field-Marshal Kazım Pasha, the Head of the Railway Construction Project

Field-Marshal Kazım Pasha, the Head of the Hejaz Railway Construction, was known for his organizational skills, prudence, and vigor. The troops, engineering staff, contractors, and workers were all subject to his orders. Kazım Pasha successfully coordinated military and civil groups together until the end, although military and civil factions were in a constant state of friction[106]. Nevertheless, this military and civil collaboration brought him unpopularity: Kazım Pasha was too involved in engineering matters and the British thought he had no expertise. Hence, serious consequences might have resulted from this type of interference, like the resignation of Chief Engineer Meissner. When Meissner's contract was close to expiry, it was hoped that Meissner would not make a regrettable decision and give up working for the railroad[107]. Although they did not authorize him to survey south of Medain Saleh, the Construction Department staff admitted that Meissner Pasha was crucial to the project. M. Gaudin Pasha, a foreign engineer in the Traffic Department, did not have the same reputation as Meissner. Some of his European assistants quit because the work became unbearable due to lower Turkish officials disobeying the orders they were given by the Europeans. Gaudin Pasha had been appointed will full powers, but still answered to Rıza Pasha. Gaudin was not on friendly terms with Rıza Pasha; therefore, confusion and problems followed. Muhtar Bey, surveyor and inspector on the line toward Medina, was not willing to assume a subordinate position. This discord convinced the British that other European contractors and workers would be fired and that only they would be able to keep on working. In that case, the British thought that they would continue the work toward Medina, even up to Mecca[108].

---

105 L/P&S/10/12, "W.S. Richards," Damascus, 8 February 1902.
106 L/P&S/10/12, "From Mr. G. Barclay to Sir Edward Grey (Confidential)," Istanbul, 17 November 1906 in *IOR*.
107 FO 78/5452, "From Consul W. S. Richards to Sir N. O'Conor," Damascus, 4 November 1902.
108 L/P&S/10/12, "From Mr. G. Barclay to Sir Edward Grey (Confidential)," Istanbul, 17 November 1906 in *IOR*.

Labor and Manpower

Hiring labor posed a wide array of challenges for the Hejaz Railway. The enterprise was in desperate need of funds. In order to meet this need, the Ottoman government turned to the army for labor. As in the case of Russian soldiers during the construction of the Siberian Hallway, Ottoman soldiers were recruited. Led by young officers drafted in 1901, the soldiers were assigned to locations between Muzeirib and Deraa to construct the railroad. Their first few months at work went by remarkably well, but lack of pay and some grievances interrupted the work for quite some time later on. In one particular case, only the prompt action of Kazım Pasha prevented a strike from turning into a massive mutiny over supplying the soldiers with new uniforms.

In early 1902, Meissner recommended to the Commission that it contract a portion of the work in the new sections; in return, he received instructions to call for tenders and, with the prospect of getting competitive prices, a considerable number of tenders from large railroad contractors in Europe were received. The Administration de Chemins de Fer Belges, as well, wanted to garner 300-400 kilometers of railway. The Belgian company assigned engineers for inspection in May 1902. In the end, the company failed to make a working arrangement with the Commission. The troops helped the Ottoman government overcome the shortage of labor; however, the government still had to attain contractors and workers to conduct engineering works and construct bridges, stations, and other buildings[109].

The local residents did not have experience in this type of work. Foreign assistance for managers and artisans was crucial, but foreigners were uncomfortable with the idea of living in the desert. In addition, the delayed delivery of provisions and construction material from Haifa to the railroad frontier slowed the ongoing construction. With every kilometer the line extended into the desert, there were increased difficulties since communication took longer and the need for labor and costs were constantly growing. While British authorities came up with a proposal for a short branch line south of Ma'an to extend to the sea in order to alleviate matters, Geheimer Bauret

---

[109] L/P&S/10/12, "From Mr. G. Barclay to Sir Edward Grey (Confidential)," Istanbul, 17 November 1906 in *IOR*.

Kapp von Ghrulstein suggested that the Damascus-Medina line could couple a line from Jeddah, via Mecca and Medina[110].

Survey parties, who commenced their work after the reconnoitering parties, needed similar caravans. In principle, the surveying area was divided into three zones, each covering 30-50 kilometers surveyed by different parties. Studying the sketches and plans coming from the preceding survey party, the following parties advanced, with the help of tachymeter, in adjusting the exact levels of the projected railroad line. All the parties entered the survey results into a book of measurements, which was sent directly to the manager of engineering works or to the technical bureau under his supervision. The technical bureau, which was initially in Ma'an, traveled as the railroad's construction progressed. The last zone in which the actual construction took place was divided into earthworks: making embankments, cuttings, railroad subtractions, culverts, infrastructures or bedding, sleepers, and rails[111].

Overall, the distribution of labor was well organized: infantry detachments accompanied the entire zone of construction; contractors and artisans dealt with infrastructure, i.e. the engineering works including tunnels and station buildings; and railroad battalions laid the sleepers and rails. Mostly Austrian and Italian contractors were responsible for the construction of bridges and native labor was employed in these works, especially because hiring labor was more difficult. In addition, approximately 450 Italian, Greek, Montenegrin, and other Christian workers were employed in the construction of station buildings, bridges, tunnels, culverts, and other difficult works such as rock cutting. Bridge construction halted occasionally, as it did when a 180-meter tunnel near Akhdar and a 20-arch bridge over the Ithil Valley had to be built. High-quality stones and sand made masonry and bedding easier and cheaper, but all other materials, especially those necessary for the iron-made bridges, had to be imported and it took time[112].

---

110 L/P&S/10/12, "From Mr. G. Barclay to Sir Edward Grey (Confidential)," Istanbul, 17 November 1906 in *IOR*.

111 L/P&S/10/12, "From Mr. G. Barclay to Sir Edward Grey (Confidential)," Istanbul, 17 November 1906 in *IOR*.

112 L/P&S/10/12, "From Mr. G. Barclay to Sir Edward Grey (Confidential)," Istanbul, 17 November 1906 in *IOR*.

As the line progressed further to the Hama-Aleppo section, there were fewer bridges and tunnels[113]. From Muzeirib to Deraa there were 20 small bridges, most of which were simply culverts[114]. The bridges from Jordan to Muzeirib numbered 83 and there were 141 on the entire Haifa line. Furthermore, eight tunnels had to be built with a total length of approximately 1,100 meters and special attention was given to drainage in the Yarmuk Valley. Whereas in the Jordan-Muzeirib section there were 246 aqueducts and culverts, in the Haifa section there were only 56 culverts up to the Jordan Valley[115].

The superstructure always advanced faster than the infrastructure. The contractors could not find enough workers for the infrastructure work because of the overwhelming difficulty of the work. Meanwhile, the almost unpopulated region promised no help since the Bedouins strongly refused to participate in building earthworks. Therefore, the rails were laid while the infrastructure, such as bridges, culverts, and similar structures, was postponed as were provisions[116].

A brief look at the railroad battalions, a new division of the Ottoman army[117], which actually deserve a more thorough analysis, will provide insight into how practical the Turkish improvisation got over time:

In addition to the imperial edict issued for the commencement of the railroad's construction on 1 May 1900, a second edict ordered the allocation of one railroad battalion from the army. The battalion was recruited from a group of selected men, mostly artisans, from the detachments of the 5th Army Corps in Damascus and their positions were replaced with new draftees. Engineer officers filled the officers' posts. A second railroad battalion assigned to help the construction became crucial as months wore on and more men were redrafted from the 5th Army Corps. The second battalion was ac-

---

[113] L/P&S/10/12, "From Sir N. O'Conor to Sir Edward Grey (Confidential)," Istanbul, 12 June 1906 in *IOR*.

[114] FO 78/5452, "From Consul W. S. Richards to Sir N. O'Conor," Damascus, 4 November 1902.

[115] L/P&S/10/12, "From Mr. G. Barclay to Sir Edward Grey (Confidential)," Istanbul, 17 November 1906 in *IOR*.

[116] L/P&S/10/12, "From Mr. G. Barclay to Sir Edward Grey (Confidential)," Istanbul, 17 November 1906 in *IOR*.

[117] L/P&S/10/12, "From Mr. G. Barclay to Sir Edward Grey (Confidential)," Istanbul, 17 November 1906 in *IOR*.

tive only during the construction; therefore, their positions in the army corps were unfilled. In principle, the soldiers in this battalion were still part of their corps and would report back to duty during mobilization and Railroad Battalion Number 2 was later incorporated into the army. Railroad battalion recruits joined the troops engaged in railroad construction, where they acquired their military and technical training. The front troops on the rail lines were composed of three battalions drawn from the Nizam infantry and two, railroad battalions quartered 5,000 men with permanent minor drafts. Regular military inspections of the troops at work were not carried out as long as the troops did their job fixing the line[118].

Soldiers in the Construction

Companies organized and scheduled the work and officers were assigned to specific sections of work in progress.[119]

The infantry battalions, comprised of approximately 400 infantry[120], were required to do certain jobs, such as earthworks, cuttings, embankments, and laying of the permanent way, while the railroad troops followed them, bedding, laying the rails, and finishing the masonry work, such as building bridges. Soldiers, also, conducted the majority of preliminary surveying for surveying companies. The Sappers worked in railroad workshops mainly as technicians, locksmiths, smiths, and carpenters. The telegraph unit, having established the telegraph lines along the Hejaz and Haifa railways, later operated these lines at specific stations[121].

Comprised of about 3,000 men, the Medina Garrison started its earthwork from Medina under the supervision of Turkish engineer officers and did not do any bridge work nor rail laying in the later stages of the construction[122].

---

118 L/P&S/10/12, "From Mr. G. Barclay to Sir Edward Grey (Confidential)," Istanbul, 17 November 1906 in *IOR*.

119 L/P&S/10/12, "From Mr. G. Barclay to Sir Edward Grey (Confidential)," Istanbul, 17 November 1906 in *IOR*.

120 L/P&S/10/12, "From Sir N. O'Conor to Sir Edward Grey (Confidential)," Istanbul, 12 June 1906 in *IOR*.

121 L/P&S/10/12, "From Mr. G. Barclay to Sir Edward Grey (Confidential)," Istanbul, 17 November 1906 in *IOR*.

122 L/P&S/10/12, "From Mr. G. Barclay to Sir Edward Grey (Confidential)," Istanbul, 17 November 1906 in *IOR*.

Four divisions of railroad troops involved in the substructure of the lines were divided into: one division to mark the trace, one division to lay the bedding, one division to lay sleepers, and one last division to place the rails.

The track laying was done by hand. A lightweight locomotive that followed the construction pulled the goods train with sleepers and loaded rails. This loaded train moved slowly on the line as more rails were laid on the plates, with two bolts and three screws.

The draftees typically wore regular civil clothes; they did not receive proper military training but obtained field experience after they started working.

Salaries Paid in Liras[123]:

1 lira for digging a cubic meter of earth

3 liras for digging out a meter of stony earth

2 liras for gathering a cubic meter of stones near the construction zone and piling up stones next to the railroad

1 lira for spreading a cubic meter of stones on the railroad

0.6 liras per meter of rails laid

0.6 liras for propping and putting position rails[124]

It was believed that a hard worker could dig three cubic meters of earth or a cubic meter of rocky earth per day; therefore, he could earn an additional three liras daily. In fact, other works did not offer opportunities for bigger bonuses. In a week, a working soldier could work five days with Thursday and Friday off since they were the washing day and the official Turkish holiday, respectively. Another limitation to earning extra income was the change in shifts: only two-thirds of all railroad troops could work simultaneously while the remaining one-third had to do the chores in the camp and exercise. The War Office included bonuses in the payrolls of the officers who worked in the construction and the office allocated the bonuses from the funds of the Hejaz Railway. In practice, awarding the workers with bonuses worked well, for it created greater incentive to get more work done. In spite

---

[123] At the time, the exchange rate of one Turkish lira was approximately 22.75 francs, while one British pound was equivalent to 25 francs.

[124] L/P&S/10/12, "From Mr. G. Barclay to Sir Edward Grey (Confidential)," Istanbul, 17 November 1906 in *IOR*.

of relatively good pay, it was only sound, personal financial management and a strong will that made living in the construction zones, located in inhospitable regions, bearable. With utter motivation and dedication to the holy cause of the project, workers could survive until the end of the construction. Without a strong, personal commitment, it is difficult to surmise how workers overcame the suffering that emanated from insufferable, hot summer days, radical changes in daily weather conditions, a shortage in water, and obliged to bivouac, in both summer and winter.

In 1902, a widespread cholera epidemic, which killed 100 soldiers, did not diminish the eagerness of the troops working at the site. This was important because most of the soldiers kept "under the flag" were regarded on active duty, even when the railroad construction exceeded its regular three-year duration. It was common for soldiers to serve approximately six years in the construction. Despite tempting salaries, there was an absence of alternative sources of labor and the soldiers' hard work and dedication to the construction resulted in moving 3,800,000 cubic meters of earth by 1 September 1904, which made the completion of the Hejaz Railway Project[125] possible.

Soldiers Working at the Construction

Approximately 4200 soldiers worked on the line from Damascus to al-Ula. Three battalions of soldiers were divided into five groups[126]. The soldiers from the two special railway battalions worked on the line between Akhdar and Medain Saleh and laid the actual, permanent rails and sleepers[127]. It was mainly Ottoman imperial troops engaged in the construction. Although there was a small number of workers that were drafted by contractors, they did not work beyond Oman and Ma'an[128].

---

[125] L/P&S/10/12, "From Mr. G. Barclay to Sir Edward Grey (Confidential)," Istanbul, 17 November 1906 in *IOR*.

[126] FO 78/5452, "From Consul W. S. Richards to Sir N. O'Conor," Damascus, 4 November 1902; L/P&S/10/12, From Mr. G. Barclay to Sir Edward Grey (Confidential)," Istanbul, 17 November 1906 in *IOR*.

[127] FO 78/5452, "From Consul W. S. Richards to Sir N. O'Conor," Damascus, 4 November 1902; L/P&S/10/12, "From Mr. G. Barclay to Sir Edward Grey (Confidential)," Istanbul, 17 November 1906 in *IOR*.

[128] L/P&S/10/12, "From Sir N. O'Conor to Sir Edward Grey (Confidential)," Istanbul, 12 June 1906 in *IOR*.

There were some hamlets neighboring the railroad and villages were even more scarce[129]. For instance, the construction in Zerqa was far from the village of the same name. There were two exceptions, a village of considerable size in Amman and a small township in Deraa. The further the railroad advanced into the desert, the more severe became the shortage of labor[130]. The nomadic Bedouins in the region did not make good workers, thus offering no solution to the labor shortage. In addition, the authorities preferred to have the soldiers work in the construction because the Bedouins asked for far higher wages than was reasonable[131]. Therefore, the main labor reserve was composed of soldiers with a small number of civil laborers from outside the district.

Kazım Pasha pragmatically intended to construct the line the cheapest possible way and was content with the fact that the troops worked well in the construction. Therefore, the pasha suggested, at a Railroad Commission meeting, to call the Redif of the Army Corps and employ the entire corps in the construction. Furthermore, he suggested that officials should abandon using a foreign and native work force hired by the contractors. Approved by the other members of the commission, except for the *Vali*, the provincial governor, and Meissner, the chief engineer, the pasha's proposal was accepted and sent to Istanbul for imperial sanction[132]. The figures for the troops engaged in construction at this time are the following:

Railroad Battalion No. 1: 1,200 soldiers from 1 September 1900 to 1 April 1900 (appeared in the survey only)

Railroad Battalion No. 2: 1,200 soldiers from May 1900, from spring 1904 to September 1905 (active at the Haifa Railroad)

The Sappers Company of the 5th Army Corps: 200 soldiers since May 1900

---

129 L/P&S/10/12, "From Sir N. O'Conor to Sir Edward Grey (Confidential)," Istanbul, 12 June 1906 in *IOR*; FO 78/5452, "From Consul W. S. Richards to Sir N. O'Conor," Damascus, 4 November 1902.

130 L/P&S/10/12, "From Sir N. O'Conor to Sir Edward Grey (Confidential)," Istanbul, 12 June 1906 in *IOR*; FO 78/5452, "From Consul W. S. Richards to Sir N. O'Conor," Damascus, 4 November 1902.

131 L/P&S/10/12, "From Mr. G. Barclay to Sir Edward Grey (Confidential)," Istanbul, 17 November 1906 in *IOR*.

132 FO 78/5452, "From Consul W. S. Richards to Sir N. O'Conor," Damascus, 4 November 1902.

Detachment of the Telegraph Company of the 5th Army Corps: 50 soldiers since 1 September 1901

Two battalions from 33rd Army Corps: 1,000 soldiers since 1 September 1901

Three battalions from 39th Army Corps: 1,000 soldiers since 1 September 1901

Four battalions from 33rd Army Corps: 1,000 men since 1 September 1901

Total number of soldiers working in the construction: 5,650[133]

Expenditure for the Soldiers

Headquartered in Damascus, a special administrative commission was formed to supply the troops working at the construction front. Its mission was challenging since the country did not have any nearby supplies. Therefore, sheep had to be shipped, as they were from Amman to Tabuk and to the desert stations at the railhead, a distance of nearly 300 miles. On the long, insufferable trip, sheep lost considerable weight making the shipment not very feasible[134].

The Railroad Commission paid half the expenditures and sometimes the cost of clothing for the troops. The military office "Seraskerlik" paid the salaries, clothing, and rations[135], which did not pose a heavy burden on its treasury because the costs were not high[136]. The main depot was located in Tabuk, which supplied mainly bread or hardtack, rice, sugar, and meat on rare occasions, with vegetables highly demanded. The quantity provided was often adequate, but the flour sent from Damascus was of low quality. A cook worked for the soldiers and provided the meals to the company during the expedition. Typical meals included tinned mutton with rice, and rusks. When water was in short supply, goat or sheepskins were used as bags to

---

133 L/P&S/10/12, "From Mr. G. Barclay to Sir Edward Grey," Istanbul, 17 November 1906 in *IOR*.

134 L/P&S/10/12, "From Mr. G. Barclay to Sir Edward Grey," Istanbul, 17 November 1906 in *IOR*.

135 L/P&S/10/12, "From Sir N. O'Conor to Sir Edward Grey (Confidential)," Istanbul, 12 June 1906 in *IOR*.

136 L/P&S/10/12, "From Sir N. O'Conor to Sir Edward Grey (Confidential)," Istanbul, 12 June 1906 in *IOR*; and FO 78/5452, "From Consul W. S. Richards to Sir N. O'Conor," Damascus, 4 November 1902.

carry water. A camel could carry four or five bags, each holding 30-40 liters of water. At night, the workers camped in tents[137].

Compared to European standards of the time, the Hejaz Railway was remarkably less expensive. The reason for its relative low cost had, in large degree, to do with its spatial context. For instance, the construction of the Damascus-Deraa line cost 1,660 liras per kilometer, or less than 2,410 liras per mile[138], and construction in the Yarmuk Valley, including the purchase of rolling stock, cost 1,400 liras. Meissner Pasha had estimated that the construction of the whole line cost 3,000,000 liras up to that point[139], but the statistics later revealed that 50,000 francs per kilometer were spent, excluding the spending related to the troops employed on the lines[140].

However, the cost of the construction was high between Mudawwara and Mecca on a number of occasions, due to the reasons listed below:

1. The railroad had to pass through arid lands that lacked and were far from any water source. Therefore, supplying water for the construction and workers posed enormous difficulties, thus considerably increasing the costs. Furthermore, an adequate supply of water had to be reserved, a year in advance, for the construction between Ma'an and Medina. Two methods were used: first, water was processed, mainly through boiling, a year before the construction reached a region without water. Second, covered cisterns were built to minimize evaporation in regions where rainfall could be collected. Water processing and preservation were extremely important: the construction program could come to a halt in the absence of an adequate water supply.

2. There were no settlements near the construction zones, as was the case between Mudawwara and Medina. Since there was no hope of including the nomadic Bedouins of the region in the construction

---

137 L/P&S/10/12, "From Mr. G. Barclay to Sir Edward Grey (Confidential)," Istanbul, 17 November 1906 in *IOR*.

138 FO 78/5452, "From Consul W. S. Richards to Sir N. O'Conor," Damascus, 4 November 1902.

139 L/P&S/10/12, "From Mr. G. Barclay to Sir Edward Grey (Confidential)," Istanbul, 17 November 1906 in *IOR*.

140 L/P&S/10/12, "From Sir N. O'Conor to Sir Edward Grey (Confidential)," Istanbul, 12 June 1906 in *IOR*.

— they demanded very high wages and were not used to this type of work — labor had to be brought in from outside.

3. Construction further into the desert required higher costs for a variety of reasons: construction material had to be transported; more locomotives, wagons, and coal were required, thus increasing the need for more labor.

4. Security costs further increased the overall expenses as a greater number of troops had to protect the workers on the line and guard the building material and other various pieces of equipment[141].

The involvement of Turkish troops in the construction and security matters helped manage, to a large extent, the aforementioned second and fourth reasons for high costs. The first and third reasons that increased the costs, however, were still pertinent until the railway approached Mecca. To counter these challenges, the Hejaz Railway was able to use a second route from Jeddah. First, the Jeddah-Mecca section was built and then the work was able to proceed through Medina to meet the main line from Damascus. In fact, Muhtar Bey strongly supported and promoted the construction of the Jeddah-Mecca section in terms of both material and spiritual aspects [142].

The British estimated that a further 1,100 kilometers of railroad had to be built by early 1906 in order to reach Mecca and that its completion would cost 60,000,000 francs, at a rate of 50,000 francs per kilometer. In order to achieve this, 150 kilometers had to be laid each year, requiring 7,500,000 francs for the entire period of eight years. In reality, the first five years of construction cost 17,500,000 francs, 3,500,000 francs per year, which was collected by donations. Specifically, the profit obtained from the sale of the animal skins sacrificed during the Eid ul-Adha and from the sale of the honorary Hejaz Railway stamps generated 16,000,000 francs, 1,000,000 francs per year. The annual income of the railroad averaged 7,500,000 francs, which was the construction cost for one year[143].

---

141 L/P&S/10/12, "From Mr. G. Barclay to Sir Edward Grey (Confidential)," Istanbul, 17 November 1906 in *IOR*.

142 L/P&S/10/12, "From Mr. G. Barclay to Sir Edward Grey (Confidential)," Istanbul, 17 November 1906 in *IOR*.

143 L/P&S/10/12, "From Sir N. O'Conor to Sir Edward Grey (Confidential)," Istanbul, 12 June 1906 in *IOR*.

The soldiers received their regular salaries for their work during the entire period of the construction of the Hejaz Railway. In addition, they received bonuses. The troops camped in tents on both sides of the railroad and moved along with the progress of construction. Although the railroads rarely passed through residential settlements, the soldiers, when it occurred, were not allowed to stay in residential areas. Each battalion and company camped separately, ate their meals, prepared by their army cooks, together, and baked their bread in portable camp ovens. The soldiers typically wore uniforms in winter and white linen suits in summer, as well as the Arab kettije, which protected them from the sun[144].

As mentioned above, the soldiers and their officers obtained decent bonuses[145]. The following scale of bonuses was given based on the following tasks:

Bonuses in Piasters:

1 cubic meter of earth: 1

1 cubic meter of rock: 2

Collecting 1 cubic meter of stones: 2

Spreading 1 cubic meter of earth on the railroad: 1

These bonuses were actually higher than the daily military wage. The bonuses were paid fairly regularly and a construction worker had the chance to make a sum of 15-20 liras at the end of his three-year work period, a satisfactory sum for the standard of the time and enough of an inducement for recruits. Although the payrolls were sometimes delayed, the Hejaz Railway fund eventually paid the bonuses, while the 5th Army Corps administration in Damascus paid the regular wages. Workers, especially in the south of Ma'an, received bonus payments; therefore, a regular worker made up to 150 piasters a month[146]. All such payments were put into a construction account[147].

---

144 L/P&S/10/12, "From Mr. G. Barclay to Sir Edward Grey (Confidential)," Istanbul, 17 November 1906 in *IOR*.

145 L/P&S/10/12, "From Sir N. O'Conor to Sir Edward Grey (Confidential)," Istanbul, 12 June 1906 and 25 September 1907 in *IOR*.

146 L/P&S/10/12, "From Mr. G. Barclay to Sir Edward Grey (Confidential)," Istanbul, 17 November 1906 in *IOR*.

147 L/P&S/10/12, "From Sir N. O'Conor to Sir Edward Grey (Confidential)," Istanbul, 12 June 1906 in *IOR*.

Pace of the Construction

The speed of the Hejaz railroad's construction was remarkable, especially considering the fact that the construction had to cover the long distance from Damascus all the way to Mecca and that this required bridges, tunnels, and many other heavy structures to be built along the way[148].

The involvement of troops in the construction, under the imperial railroad administration, was an invaluable contribution to the momentum of the construction[149]. It is a well-known fact that their hard work made this project possible. For instance, in the summer of 1900, the Mudawwara-Zat al-Hajj section was completed and, in late 1900, the lines reached as far as the Tabuk Station[150]. Incentives for the soldiers, as well as their emotional attachment to the work, included among others the appointment of Meissner Pasha as the Chief Engineer and Director of the project, and his effort, associated with the support of the High Commission, in ensuring the timely salary payment to the employees[151].

In early 1902, there was great momentum to progress with the construction. Meissner Pasha's energy and administrative competence encompassed the entire initiative; the soldiers, in particular, had gained experience constructing the lines and this increased their work capacity to lay two to three kilometers per line. In addition, this period saw an incredible increase in skilled labor[152]: for instance, the workers at the Riyaq-Hama construction site completed the section very quickly and were assigned, immediately, to finish the outstanding construction sites of the Hejaz Railway. Towards the end of spring that year, however, the pilgrims' return from the Hajj contributed to the spread of a cholera epidemic among the soldiers and other workers in Amman, a central construction site, precipitating a call for a break in work that lasted seven months. Meanwhile, the Commission agreed with the

---

148 L/P&S/10/12, "From Sir N. O'Conor to Sir Edward Grey (Confidential)," Istanbul, 25 September 1907 in *IOR*.

149 L/P&S/10/12, "From Sir N. O'Conor to Sir Edward Grey (Confidential)," Istanbul, 12 June 1906 in *IOR*.

150 L/P&S/10/12, "From Mr. G. Barclay to Sir Edward Grey (Confidential)," Istanbul, 17 November 1906 in *IOR*.

151 L/P&S/10/12, "From Sir N. O'Conor to Sir Edward Grey (Confidential)," Istanbul, 12 June 1906 in *IOR*.

152 L/P&S/10/12, "From Mr. G. Barclay to Sir Edward Grey (Confidential)," Istanbul, 17 November 1906 in *IOR*.

French Company on the payment of an indemnity/compensation. In 1903, the 330 kilometers of railroad between Damascus and Deraa went into service. Although the train service was irregular at best, it facilitated the transportation of railroad materials all the way to Deraa. However, the line was too far south to bear the heavy freight expenses of the materials on the Beirut-Damascus line and from Damascus to Amman; thus there were serious considerations to build a branch line from Deraa to Haifa[153].

According to the plan, the Ma'an-Mudawwara section, which was 113.2 kilometers, would be opened in order to assist the pilgrimage to Mecca that year[154]. In late 1905, 572 kilometers of the line were completed up to Mudawwara. From 1 September 1900 to that year, the rails were laid between Tabuk and al-Ula, 30 kilometers south of Medain Saleh. Furthermore, the earthworks 40 kilometers outside of al-Ula were completed, while an additional 44 kilometers were cleared for work. In Medina, at the other end, four kilometers were completed by then and 46 kilometers were about to be laid[155]. The progress of the construction, considering the size of the project, was remarkable[156]. In particular, the infantry battalions processed 80,000 cubic meters of earth in only five months[157]. The battalions worked, on average, two to three kilometers a day[158], and even one kilometer on special occasions[159], which indicates the amount of experience they gained. As a re-

---

153 L/P&S/10/12, "From Sir N. O'Conor to Sir Edward Grey (Confidential)," Istanbul, 12 June 1906 in *IOR*.

154 L/P&S/10/12, "From Mr. G. Barclay to Sir Edward Grey (Confidential)," Istanbul, 17 November 1906 in *IOR*.

155 L/P&S/10/12, "Sir N. O'Conor to Sir Edward Grey," Istanbul, 25 September 1907 in *IOR*; The stations, both proposed and already built, were the following: Tabuk on the 692nd kilometer, Valley Athel on the 720th, Dar al-Haj on the 741st, Mustabka on the 755th, Hamis on the 782nd, Dezad on the 805th, Muazzam on the 828th, Hishm-Sana on the 853rd, Dar al-Hamra on the 880th, Al-Mutaab on the 904th, Abu-Taker on the 918th, Al-Mushim on the 930th, Medain Saleh on the 953rd, and Al-Ula on about the 980th. L/P&S/10/12, "Sir N. O'Conor to Sir Edward Grey," Istanbul, 25 September 1907 in *IOR*.

156 L/P&S/10/12, "Sir N. O'Conor to Sir Edward Grey," Istanbul, 12 June 1906 in *IOR*; and FO 78/5452, "From Consul W. S. Richards to Sir N. O'Conor," Damascus, 4 November 1902.

157 L/P&S/10/12, "From Sir N. O'Conor to Sir Edward Grey (Confidential)," Istanbul, 12 June 1906 in *IOR*.

158 Ottoman troops, such as the troop between Medain and al-Ula, could pave up to four kilometers of rails a day; see L/P&S/10/12, "Sir N. O'Conor to Sir Edward Grey," Istanbul, 25 September 1907 in *IOR*.

159 L/P&S/10/12, "From Mr. G. Barclay to Sir Edward Grey (Confidential)," Istanbul, 17 November 1906 in *IOR*.

sult of the construction's rapid progress, Meissner estimated that the Deraa-Jordan Valley section, between Damascus and Amman, would be completed in 14-16 months[160].

Between Damascus and Amman there were four finished stations: Deraa, Muzeirib, Nessib, and Mafraq. Three other stations, Khirbet al-Samra, Zerqa, and Amman, were almost complete.

Beyond Amman, the rails were laid up to Deba'a, 66 kilometers away. After Deba'a, the earthwork was completed up to Qatrana, 38 kilometers away, while construction was in progress 70 kilometers up to Uneiza. In total, 303 kilometers of the railroad were laid, and 108 kilometers of railroad were under construction[161].

The distance between Muzeirib and Ma'an was 800 kilometers, one-third of the entire line. As on 1 September 1902, the average annual work of construction recorded was 200 kilometers, a remarkable achievement for the time[162]. Although the construction between Muzeirib and Deraa began in 1900, the progress was slower because of a number of technical difficulties[163]. Due to the poor progress of the construction in the region, the High Commission secured the necessary financial means to purchase materials and undertake the construction more effectively; as a result, they expected an advance of 150-kilometers per year[164]. This was a turning point in the history of the construction in that region: the high quality material and the priority it received from the administration resulted in satisfactory, unwavering advancement in the construction.

One of the main reasons for the increased rate of construction was the promotion of Chief Engineer Meissner Pasha to Engineering Manager, in January 1901. Another reason was the emotional attachment of all involved in the project: the officials and workers together wished that this noble work, which invited the countenance of God and appreciation of the Proph-

---

[160] L/P&S/10/12, "Consul Richards to Sir N. O'Conor," Damascus, 15 December 1903 in *IOR*.

[161] L/P&S/10/12, "Consul Richards to Sir N. O'Conor," Damascus, 15 December 1903 in *IOR*.

[162] FO 78/5452, "From Consul W. S. Richards to Sir N. O'Conor," 10 November 1902.

[163] L/P&S/10/12, From Mr. G. Barclay to Sir Edward Grey (Confidential)," Istanbul, 17 November 1906 in *IOR*.

[164] L/P&S/10/12, "From Sir N. O'Conor to Sir Edward Grey (Confidential)," Istanbul, 12 June 1906 in *IOR*.

et, would materialize soon. Apparently, all these factors were a driving force behind the remarkable pace that the construction assumed[165].

Sultan Abdulhamid II favored and admired the planned railway from Damascus to Mecca, mainly because the railway would facilitate the pilgrimage to Mecca, the Holy City[166]. Another incentive to speed up the construction came from the sultan: he ordered the line to extend quickly to Ma'an by 1 September 1903, the 27th anniversary of his accession to the throne[167]. His orders and efforts provided an impetus to accomplish the project[168]: he expressed his candid wish that the line rapidly reach as far as Medain Saleh, motivating all those involved in the construction[169].

While Abdulhamid II put his efforts into giving momentum to the construction and completion of the project, he also tried to raise public interest for the railway among the people of Medina to show its advantages over the traditional camel caravans. In the latter endeavor, the notable sheikhs of Medina and surrounding area were invited, in early August 1906, to Erasiman, and they traveled by railway to Damascus with all their expenses paid by the Ottoman government by the order of the Sultan. This generous gesture from the Ottoman Sultan showed that the he was considerate and concerned about the future of the railway[170].

The following is a list of the completed lines as of January 1906[171]:

Kilometers Covered:

The main line from Damascus to Mudawwara: 572

Between Mudawwara and Zat al-Hajj: approximately 17

The branch line from Haifa to Deraa: 161

Total kilometers covered: 750

---

165 L/P&S/10/12, "From Mr. G. Barclay to Sir Edward Grey (Confidential)," Istanbul, 17 November 1906 in *IOR*.

166 FO 78/5452, "H.R. O'Conor," Istanbul, 23 May 1900.

167 FO 78/5452, "From Consul W. S. Richards to Sir N. O'Conor," 10 November 1902.

168 L/P&S/10/12, "From Mr. G. Barclay to Sir Edward Grey (Confidential)," Istanbul, 17 November 1906 in *IOR*.

169 L/P&S/10/12, "From U.F.S. (H.R.O'Conor) to Foreign Office," Therapia, 6 August 1906 in *IOR*.

170 L/P&S/10/12, "From U.F.S. (H.R.O'Conor) to Foreign Office," Therapia, 6 August 1906 in *IOR*.

171 L/P&S/10/12, "From Mr. G. Barclay to Sir Edward Grey (Confidential)," Istanbul, 17 November 1906 in *IOR*.

In August 1906, the construction reached Dar al-Hamra, 870 kilometers from Damascus[172], with an average of 144 kilometers per year. These figures show that the Hejaz Railway was progressing well and quickly, at a rate of 150 kilometers a year, which was a remarkable pace[173]. Compared to the original estimates that 200 kilometers could be laid each year, the actual figures were lower but still significant, considering regional and other certain attributes, such as a lack of settlements, scarcity of water[174], the earlier interruptions caused by the long negotiations with the French Railroad Company on the Damascus-Muzeirib line, and lengthy delays in the delivery of sleepers and rails.

Anatolian railroad construction averaged less than 150 kilometers per year; the reason that construction took more was because the railroads in Anatolia were nominal-gauge railroads, whereas the Hejaz Railway consisted of narrow-gauge rails. In September 1903, the year before the costly construction in the Yarmuk Valley began, the expenses for the Hejaz Railroad, including rolling stock, station buildings, etc. amounted to 1,500 liras, or approximately 35,000 piasters per kilometer. In late 1905, the balance sheets prepared after the completion of the section through the Yarmuk Valley indicated an increase to 2,200 liras, or approximately 50,000 piasters per kilometer. An analysis of the figures, even with the higher costs noted in 1905, shows that the cost of construction of the Hejaz Railway was relatively lower. The main reason for its low cost was related to the assistance received from Turkish troops in the construction process[175]. As a result of the aforementioned reasons, the Hejaz Railway was successfully launched within eight years[176].

Disease

Caused by abrupt changes in weather conditions or malnutrition, disease was a daunting challenge to the construction process. Dysentery, typhoid, and scurvy were endemic especially accompanied by malnutrition and a lack

---

[172] L/P&S/10/12, "From U.F.S. (H.R.O'Conor) to Foreign Office," Therapia, 6 August 1906 in *IOR*.

[173] L/P&S/10/12, "From Sir N. O'Conor to Sir Edward Grey (Confidential)," Istanbul, 12 June 1906 in *IOR*.

[174] L/P&S/10/12, "Consul Richards to Sir N. O'Conor," Damascus, 15 December 1903 in *IOR*.

[175] L/P&S/10/12, "From Mr. G. Barclay to Sir Edward Grey (Confidential)," Istanbul, 17 November 1906 in *IOR*.

[176] L/P&S/10/12, "From Sir N. O'Conor to Sir Edward Grey (Confidential)," Istanbul, 12 June 1906 in *IOR*.

of green vegetables in addition to the hot climate. Italian engineers proved that green vegetables could grow in the Tabuk Oasis, but no further steps were taken to supply the troops with them. Unlike the soldiers, the foreign workers adjusted to the local conditions, with food provided by their contractors. Under these harsh conditions, sick workers, departing the construction zone, packed the returning trains[177]. Because of disease and other related issues, the number of workers on active duty did not exceed 3,300[178]. To counter the health problems, military hospitals with 150 beds were built in Tabuk and al-Ula. There was a temporary hut hospital in Ma'an with 150 beds; however, severe patients were sent to Damascus. In Ma'an, the sick waited in line on open platform wagons without medical care[179].

"RAILONOMICS:" FINANCIAL DIMENSIONS OF THE HEJAZ RAILWAY PROJECT

Revenue Sources

Muslims regarded financing the Hejaz Project as a religious duty, which united them under the same objective[180]. With this goal in mind, the authorities appealed to the generosity of Muslims to support the project[181].

An extensive series of announcements called on the Muslim community to make donations in order to finance the project. The Ottoman government turned to the notables, distinguished local and religious leaders, and asked for their support in the project. Furthermore, speeches were given on the religious nature and importance of the construction and the difference the Hejaz Railway would make in facilitating the holy pilgrimage. For example, the speech Seyyid Abdul Hak Effendi of Baghdad gave in Amritsa emphasized the necessity of all Muslims' supporting this holy undertaking by any means available[182].

---

177 L/P&S/10/12, "From Mr. G. Barclay to Sir Edward Grey (Confidential)," Istanbul, 17 November 1906 in *IOR*.

178 FO 78/5452, "From Consul W. S. Richards to Sir N. O'Conor," Damascus, 4 November 1902.

179 L/P&S/10/12, "From Mr. G. Barclay to Sir Edward Grey (Confidential)," Istanbul, 17 November 1906 in *IOR*.

180 L/P&S/10/12, "From Sir N. O'Conor to Sir Edward Grey," Therapia, 18 September 1907 in *IOR*.

181 FO 78/5452, "From Consul W. S. Richards to Sir N. O'Conor," 10 November 1902.

182 FO 78/5452, "Marquess of Lansdowne, K.G.," Istanbul, 30 November 1900.

In response to the far-reaching campaign to gain support for the Hejaz Railway project, Indian Muslims contributed 5,000,000 rupees to the Hejaz Railway Fund. In addition, the Muslims of the State of Hyderabad proposed to be taxed 6.25 per cent. This tax on their wealth would produce another 5,000,000 rupees, but they wanted to determine how their tax payments would be spent: they stated that three-fifths of it should pay for the construction of a branch line to connect Jeddah and Mount Arafat, 60 miles from Mecca, and the remaining two-fifths should be deposited into the general railroad fund[183]. In this respect, the financial responsibility of the construction was shared, to a large degree, by the entire Muslim world[184], while it was the Ottoman Turks who led and managed the project, finished its construction, and organized the Muslim world to finance the project.

The generous donations of Muslims eventually reached a total of 750,000 liras. In addition, there were various sources of revenue specially established to form the Hejaz Railway Fund. Although there are many, the following short list gives an indication of the sources that financed the Hejaz Railway Fund[185]:

1. A poll-tax of 5 piasters for every head of a Muslim family in the Ottoman Empire, which would yield 100,000 piasters per year, was levied.

2. The Tax, levied on a sliding scale was based on honorific distinctions. Competition for decorations was high; therefore, this tax was supposed to generate a significant revenue source.

3. Half the taxes on charcoal and wood totaled approximately 50,000 liras per year.

4. The tax on stamps required a 1-piaster stamp on official petitions and other documents.

5. The tax on official stamps of different prices, were mandatory on documents related to house rentals, contracts, leases, etc.

---

[183] L/P&S/10/12, "Consul Richards to Sir N. O'Conor," Damascus, 15 December 1903 in *IOR*.

[184] L/P&S/10/12, "From Sir N. O'Conor to Sir Edward Grey," Therapia, 18 September 1907 in *IOR*.

[185] L/P&S/10/12, "From Mr. G. Barclay to Sir Edward Grey (Confidential)," Istanbul, 17 November 1906 in *IOR*; and L/P&S/10/12, "Consul Richards to Sir N. O'Conor," Damascus, 15 December 1903 in *IOR*.

6. A Property tax of one percent of the value of land and buildings for
    sale was acquired in return for the title deeds, which was approved
    by the authorities of the *Tapu* Department, i.e. Land Registry.

7. The tax on stamps, a 1-piaster stamp, which had to accompany *il-
    mühaber*, i.e. a certificate of proof, issued by the *muhtar*, the head
    of a village, and members of the village council of elders.

8. The tax on land or property for sale. A certain percentage was re-
    quired as a tax on the property when sold on a provisional "*hoca,*"
    title deed.

9. The sale of animal skins donated during Eid ul-Adha.

10. The sales of fancy cigarette cases made of gelatin and sold by agents
    of the Tobacco Régie for 20 liras per case, separate from the cost
    of the enclosed cigarettes.

11. The revenue earned from the net receipts of the line open to traffic,
    1,000 liras (gross receipts) per month[186].

In numerous other ways, the levy of the Hejaz Railroad stamps collected money from the Ottoman Muslim community. Although this strategy of
raising money for the Hejaz Railway was a burden on Muslims, no one pe-
titioned their objections or withheld paying their dues, because they, apparently, believed in the religious importance of the project. The British estimated that the sources of revenue would generate a considerable annual sum
of money, at least 250,000 liras. The accumulated sum would, at least, cover all the expenses of the construction. In case the sum exceeded the basic
expenses, the outstanding balance would be used to purchase rolling stock
and other additional materials to facilitate the construction[187].

The revenue collected from certain government enforcements, such as
stamp duties and the sales of animal skins during Eid ul-Adha, were successfully allocated to the Hejaz Railway Fund[188].

Other sources of revenue were available, as well. For instance, the pro-
ceeds of phosphate deposits, near al-Salt on the Hejaz line, and the sulfur de-

---

[186] Ibid; L/P&S/10/12, "From Mr. G. Barclay to Sir Edward Grey (Confidential)," Istanbul, 17
      November 1906 in *IOR*.

[187] Ibid; and L/P&S/10/12, "Consul Richards to Sir N. O'Conor," Damascus, 15 December
      1903 in *IOR*.

[188] Ibid.

posits, near Hamma on the Haifa-Deraa branch line, were at the disposal of the Hejaz Railway administration[189].

Another source in the service of the Hejaz Railway Project was the receipts. In 1905, the receipts generated nearly 100,000 liras and the traffic receipts paid on the sections to Amman covered the operating expenses of the whole line up to Ma'an, excluding the southern extension to Tabuk, which was under military administration. The revenue generated by the Hejaz railroad, stamp taxes, and other sources amounted, Meissner Pasha estimated, to 350,000 liras, or 8,750,000 francs, per year, an amount that could cover the costs of the construction. The following plans were drawn up for financial arrangements:

1. The organization of the building authorities and of the Directors
2. The introduction of negotiations for the acquisition of territory
3. An extensive survey of the line to make a general construction plan
4. The procurement of railroad materials[190]

Significantly, the Hejaz Railway succeeded in devising various ways and means to fund the construction. On 1 September 1905, the income equaled 46.7 million francs, at a rate of 7.5 million francs per year. Moreover, the Railway administration would have a sum of 8.25 million francs as credit after paying off all its debts. For instance, a balance sheet in 1905 shows a surplus of 27,524,274 piasters, approximately 230,000 liras. The total income amounted to 252,237,621 piasters with expenditures no more than 224,713,347 piasters. A total amount of 92,054,773 piasters was collected from miscellaneous sources of revenue and allocated to the Hejaz Railway, 88,448,101 piasters from donations, 30,399,301 piasters from imperial subsidies under the "Banque Agricole", and 36,999,127 piasters from profits on money exchanges in provinces. The income from completed sections that were open to traffic, mainly the Haifa branch, was 6,190,336 piasters, which came almost entirely from the transportation of materials to the construction zone. The taxes levied on the districts of the railroad generated 1,467,505 piasters. The total expenditure would have been 2,211,080 liras, but 97,200 liras had to be deducted because 5,000 tons of sleepers and 11,000 tons of rails were not used yet. In addition,

---

[189] Ibid.
[190] Ibid.

79,436 liras were charged on a checking account, even though they had to be considered part of the operating costs[191].

The figures given above show the huge amount of money raised and spent on the Hejaz Railway. From the launch of the lines to September 1905, an additional 46.7 million francs were raised, which suggests that the Ottoman Sultan did not want the Hejaz Railway Fund to suffer from a lack of income. Furthermore, the interest that the construction accumulated later, removed earlier concerns regarding whether or not the funds would be sufficient to maintain the lines. Auler Pasha's opinions and predictions on financial matters were very optimistic as he based his opinions essentially on the information and facts presented by İzzet Pasha, the Secretary of the Sultan and manager of the Hejaz Railway Project. Despite his strong optimism, Auler Pasha's estimate on the lucrative capacity of the line, up to Ma'an, and the promising future of the Hanran, with its rich mineral and agricultural sources, would provide enough support to keep the Hejaz Railway functioning. However, there were shortcomings: the trains ran once a week and had to move at a low speed because the gauges were very narrow and the entire operation had to rely on revenue collected from taxes and other sources. As a result, Auler Pasha suggested transporting the pilgrims to Mecca free of charge. Even if this occurred, the pilgrims, and the broader Muslim community, would be asked to support the railway in one form or another[192].

At the end of July 1906, the income, cash reserves, and expenses of the Hamidiye Hejaz Railway were the following[193]:

Receipts

Revenues Indicated in Piaster
1. Contributions: 88,448,161 39
2. Various receipts: 92,054,773 29½
3. Contributions of the Bank of Agriculture: 30,399,301 14
4. Profit on money exchanged from foreign currency where available: 36,999,127 15

---

191 Ibid.
192 Ibid.
193 L/P&S/10/12, "Consul Richards to Sir N. O'Conor," Damascus, 15 December 1903 in *IOR*.

5. Transportation of passengers and goods on the rail lines at the Haifa branch: 6,190,336 16½
6. Provincial contributions to the lines etc.: 1,467,505 26½
7. Pension income from the workers on the lines: 100,813 14
8. Deposits from the auctions of the various factories etc.: 1,816,787 38
    Total revenues collected: 237,476,807 32½

In addition,

Converting the Mejidie to 19 piasters and the lira to 102 piasters, with a 30-piaster currency disparity in the contributions and other incomes, and converting the lira to 100 piasters for spending, equaled a sum to be added: 4,239,186 4½

Cumulative sum: 257,176, 807 32½

Expenses

The following are the wages and related expenses paid during the Hejaz Railway's construction.

Expenses in Piasters:

1. Rails, splinters, parquets, and iron-made objects: 37,563,185 1
2. Locomotives, wagons, baggage wagons (fourgons): 16,877,183 11½
3. Engineering and technical instruments, balancing bridges, stone-breaking machinery, etc.: 3,316,971 32
4. Steel and wooden cross-bars, etc.: 26,652,018 38
5. Hydraulic lime, cement, telegraphic wire, and other wooden materials: 4,958,414 5½
6. Salaries: 11,827,295 13
7. Travel expenses: 320,266 3
    [Total carried in advance: 101,515,334 29]
8. Amounts paid for the purchase contracts and deposit of lime bags: 2,230,294 21
9. Customs paid to the Beirut Port Company for the shipment of railroad materials: 484,521 0
10. Construction expenses paid for technical operations, soil leveling, rail placing, and bonuses to the officers and soldiers: 116,877,861 37½
    Total: 221,108,012 8½

Expenses for accounting, administering, and distributing salaries, purchases, and other general expenses: 7,943,620 2

Balance......: 213,164,392 6½

Expenses for the Haifa line: 56,298,914 0

Expenses for the Great Hejaz line: 147,141,478 6½

203,440,392 6½

Rails and cross-bars in stock: 9,724,000 0

Total: 213,164,392 6½

Expenses not directly related to the construction:

1. Printing, transportation, and expenses to collect donations and profits: 1,120,712 28

2. Freight and insurance payments for foreign currency exchange with Mejidies where applicable: 670,700 11

3. Cost of producing honorary railroad medals: 170,998 2

4. Payments made to the agreed accounts, from the fire contributions, and to Haramayn, the Holy Cities of Islam: 1,636,924 17

Total: 3,605,355 18

Previous calculated expenses: 221,108,012 8½

Grand total of expenses: 224,713, 347 26½

1. Available amount in the account at the Ottoman Imperial Bank: 22,792,324 23

2. Amount available from the Ministry of Finance: 790,108 10½

3. Available amount in the account at the Bank of Agriculture: 2,596,534 18½

4. Credit, available in small quantities but not cashed yet, at the Ottoman Imperial Bank: 422,108 29

5. Amount available in the Committee of Syria: 1,450,971 18½

6. Pensions available in the account at the Bank of Agriculture: 95,115 32

7. Equivalent of foreign exchange made at the Imperial Minting House: 148,166 34

8. Cash available in Yemen to convert foreign currency: 228,941 35

28,524,274 1½

Total funds: 253,237,621 28½

Total expenses: 221,713,317 26½

Amount available after balance: 28,524, 274 1½

The British predicted that a lack of funds would not cause the project to halt. If the Hejaz Railway needed further financial backing, they believed that the Ottoman government had the means to provide the necessary financial support[194].

POLITICAL PROBLEMS

Locals' Perceptions of the Hejaz Railway

A major challenge to railway in the Hejaz region came from the people whose living was related to the pilgrimage route and the camel caravans.

The district of al-Leja, which the railroad intersected between Mismia and Deraa, contained lava masses from the mountains of Jabal Druz, which stood 30-40 feet below ground level. Some fugitives hid in this region, making it unsafe for travelers. However, they did not try to attack the rail lines, thanks to the garrison in Mismia. The Druzes of the Jabal Druz were quiescent and their trade in corn and other produce reached the Ezra and Ghazala stations near Deraa. The Druzes were well armed with, reportedly, 10,000 rifles, namely Martinis, some Gras, and Berdan. Like the Druzes, the residents of the Hanran Plain were strong and warlike and armed with quite a few Martini rifles. It was not uncommon for travelers in the region to come across a group of mounted men with Martinis. These men lived in villages and cultivated the fertile lands that served as a granary for Damascus and a source of agricultural exports for Haifa.

The Adwan and Banu Sakhr were located near al-Salt and further north, respectively. While the Banu Sakhr's sheikh was Reimih ibn Fais, the Adwan was led by Sheikh Ali Diab and Sheikh al-Sultan, his son. The Roalla and Aneize, two other eminent tribes in the east of the desert, rarely came near the line. However, opposition to the railway was very strong, particularly in southern Tabuk.

The Ibn al-Fadi tribe lived between Medina and the coast. When the Ibn al-Fadi chose to side with the government against the hostile tribes and

---

194 L/P&S/10/12, "Consul Richards to Sir N. O'Conor," Damascus, 15 December 1903 in *IOR*.

worked in the interests of the railway, the Ottoman government praised their efforts, rewarding their sheikh with the title of Pasha[195].

The local governor, the Sheikh of Rabigh, supported the railway project as well. Consequently, Rabigh and his tribe benefited from the growing social and commercial activity that came with the railroad. However, Jeddah lost much of its prestige and activity for two reasons: the railroad did not have a stop in Jeddah and the import of wheat and barley deprived Jeddah of its commercial profits when it changed its overland course to the sea route. In addition, barley, an essential source of food for the camels on the pilgrimage, was imported since it was not needed in the absence of business[196].

The Attacks and their Objectives

The people with vested interest in camel transport from Medina to Mecca and the coast, were alarmed when they learned that the Ottoman government used steamers to ship railroad material to Rabigh, where the construction of a port was soon to begin. The discontent arguably stemmed from the losses caused by the construction of the line, since the Yanbu Road was almost entirely abandoned, and Medina visitors took the Haifa or Damascus road and reached Medina by train[197].

The aggressive activities of some tribes continued to grow near Medina. In the winter of 1908, they attacked the rail lines and the guards, and it caused losses on both sides. The insurgents targeted the railroad up to the Hadiyya Station, 170 kilometers from Medina, and removed the sleepers and rails for one kilometer and carried them away. Although the Turkish authorities repaired the damage, the aggression continued. Kazım Pasha, the Müşir in charge of railroad construction in the Hejaz, rushed to Medina. Between 10 and 11 January 1908, Kazım Pasha travelled from Medina to Rabigh with a large escort of over 1,000 cavalry. On the way, the soldiers were attacked in Bir al-Mashi, ten hours from Medina: While the attackers killed eight to nine soldiers and wounded several more, they lost three men. Later,

---

[195] L/P&S/10/12, "From Mr. G. Barclay to Sir Edward Grey (Confidential)," Istanbul, 17 November 1906 in *IOR*.

[196] L/P&S/10/12, "Sir N. O'Conor to Sir Edward Grey," Istanbul, 18 February 1908 in *IOR*.

[197] L/P&S/10/12, "From Mr. G. Barclay to Sir Edward Grey (Confidential)," Istanbul, 17 November 1906 in *IOR*.

during the *eid*, the religious holiday on 11 January 1908, Kazım Pasha went to Mecca and attended the holiday ceremony. From Mecca, he wired a message to the Palace in Istanbul and requested back up. This incident caused the closure of the pilgrimage route from Yanbu to Medina. Kazım Pasha captured eight sheikhs suspected of leading the attack, but orders from Istanbul requested that they be released. The pasha released them, opened the pilgrimage route, and the first large caravan after the incident left Yanbu with 6,000 camels[198].

In another instance, a large mob engaged a night attack against a Turkish soldier camp in Bir Rumah, about two miles from Medina, but the soldiers repulsed them, inflicting heavy casualties. In fact, Turkish officials received intelligence reports on the attack several hours beforehand and ordered the troops to light the cane lights at sunset as usual, leave the tents, and set an ambush on the hills around the camp when it turned dark. To the troops' credit, the execution of the order was flawless: at around 11 pm, 1,000-1,500 raiders rushed the camp from all sides. Unaware of the situation, they found themselves in a deserted camp under heavy fire from the surrounding hills. Reportedly, 300-350 attackers were killed and wounded and the rest ran for their lives, leaving approximately 500 rifles behind[199].

The attacks on the Hejaz Railway continued in northern Medina. Nevertheless, the rail lines were quickly repaired, regardless of the cost, each time they were incapacitated. On one occasion, soldiers protecting the line near Medina came under attack, with several killed and some wounded[200]. After twenty days, the railroad between Yanbu and Medina was back in business and three or four large caravans loaded with merchandise used it with success.

The last caravan left Yanbu—the 23rd incident in the reports— and failed to travel through: two days after they left Yanbu, the camel riders received news that an armed group had blockaded the road in Medman near Medina and the caravan had to stop. After negotiations, the caravan was permitted to continue. The Jeddah-Mecca road, safe from attacks for a short time, came under a robbery assault—the 26th incident in the report—when a caravan with 35 loaded camels was approximately ten miles from Jeddah,

---

198 L/P&S/10/12, "Sir N. O'Conor to Sir Edward Grey," Istanbul, 18 February 1908 in *IOR*.
199 FO 195/2286, "Acting British Consul, Charge de Affaires," Istanbul, 30 July 1908.
200 FO 195/2286, "Charge d'Affairs, (J.H.McMahan, Consul, Jeddah)," Istanbul, 17 August 1908.

a location conducive to attacks. It was seized and sugar and other commodities that the caravan carried under Turkish ownership were usurped[201].

The nature and extent of the attacks against the *dhaws*, large sailing ships at the port, suggest that the attacks not only focused on the Hejaz Railway but also targeted the whole region. In one instance, a dhaw loaded with grain, left Lohaya on the Yemen coast on the twentieth of the previous month. On one morning—the first incident in the reports—the dhaw was attacked while it was anchored at Moajjiz near Shageg, between Lohaya and Confidah. The pirates released the captain and his six crew members and freed the ship only after seizing the goods.

The owner, a British Indian, notified the British consulate in Jeddah about the incident and requested 241 sterlings in compensation. The British representative discussed the matter with Ahmed Pasha in Jedda, and persuaded him to settle the owner's petition in a quick and efficient manner. In reply, Ahmed Pasha gave 20 Sterlings in order to send five sailors back to India and promised to settle the owner's petition of compensation, 241 sterlings[202], in a month.

The Policy towards the Attacks on the Railway

In an effort to sustain the momentum of construction, the central government subsidized the local sheikhs, paying them an annual honorarium to protect the lines under construction. In practice, this method worked well, especially with the Adwan and Banu Sakhr, two large tribes between Damascus and Ma'an, who were in an alliance with the authorities[203].

The Sultan's encouragement to quickly and efficiently complete the construction of the line up to Medain Saleh was well received. Illustrative of the Sultan's concern for the railroad, his orders in the form of positive reinforcement were made public to the residents of Medina. In the face of blatant and fundamentalist charges, the Sultan reassured everyone that the railroad would not make any changes other than merely supplant the mode of travel. When the line reached Tabuk, an opening ceremony was arranged in conjunction with the Sultan's birthday. Several days prior, leading sheikhs

---

201 FO 195/2286, "Acting British Consul, Charge de Affaires," Istanbul, 30 July 1908.
202 FO 195/2286, "Acting British Consul, Charge de Affaires," Istanbul, 30 July 1908.
203 L/P&S/10/12, "From Mr. G. Barclay to Sir Edward Grey (Confidential)," Istanbul, 17 November 1906 in *IOR*.

and notable officials of Tabuk and Medain Saleh met in Tabuk and took private trains along the line to Damascus. In Damascus, the Governor of Damascus and other high-ranking officials greeted them warmly. On a similar occasion, in early August 1906, the leading figures of Medina and the surrounding area came to Erasiman and took the train to Damascus, during which they enjoyed the comfort and refreshments offered by the Turkish government as the Sultan had ordered. On the way back to Tabuk, they all attended the opening ceremony, which emphasized the religious significance of the Hejaz Railway and held community prayers for the Sultan. The ceremonies met their objectives, quelling the tribal hostilities, at least until the opening of the line between Jeddah and Mecca[204]. Based on their past experience, the government took further steps against potential attacks. For instance, cavalry units were moved to various stations, guarding and regularly patrolling the railroad. In addition, two infantry regiments, mounted on camels, were mobilized to guard the telegraph lines passing through the desert from Ma'an to Medina and Aqaba. The regiments patrolled the telegraph line and inspected the wires on a regular basis, while several of the assigned soldiers made repairs along the way[205].

The station buildings in southern Tabuk were established on a special plan: they contained emergency holes for the men serving there to escape from the attacks. A typical building made of stone was 11 by 12 meters and contained four rooms, while others were a little larger with six rooms. An iron door provided the only entry into the building and led to a small courtyard next to the open windows of the common room. A masonry cistern or well, if available, was located in the courtyard. One of the rooms stored the provisions, which could last for approximately two weeks. The walls were built, including the emergency holes, eight feet above ground level. The building itself was five meters high with 50 centimeter-square windows near the roof. It was possible to climb to the flat roof from the courtyard with the help of iron battens built into the walls. The ceiling wall was 50 centimeters high with no holes, which left the holes below as the only places that attackers could shoot from. The porch in the front was also a weak location in

---

204 L/P&S/10/12, "From U.F.S. (H.R.O' Conor) to Foreign Office," Therapia, 6 August 1906 in *IOR*.

205 L/P&S/10/12, "From Mr. G. Barclay to Sir Edward Grey (Confidential)," Istanbul, 17 November 1906 in *IOR*.

terms of security. The latrine was located inside the building and used a dry-earth system.

In addition to these security measures, a special commissary was stationed in Ma'an and an infantry unit was sent there as *zaptiye*, i.e. gendarmerie. In Aqaba, there was one garrison and half a battalion from the Hejaz Division and three posts of fifty men were set up on the Aqaba route. The distance of the military units deployed is below:

Location	Distance in kilometers
Ma'an	n/a
Afule	28
Guera	40
Abu al-Hairan	28
Aqaba	20
Total	116

In Guera, there was a telegraph office and a large post, where 80 men worked. On the way to Afule there was a gradually incline toward Ma'an, and on the top of the slope, at 4,625 feet, there was a military post. There were several decent-size springs in the vicinity; in fact, ancient Roman ruins show that there used to be a settlement in the region. After the incline, the road sloped 800 feet downward, which was an extension of the Batn al-Ghul. Guera, a wide, waterless terrain, did not have anything more than small springs. Near the springs, small shrubs and some vegetables were available. The last part of the journey to Aqaba was the Valley Ithm, a mile-wide, rocky valley with several small springs[206].

British and French Railway Diplomacy

Even before the beginning of the Hejaz Railway Project's construction, it was anticipated that the project would herald a new era for Arabia. At the same time, the changes it caused revitalized the image of the Sultan in the region. The Hejaz Railroad eventually planned to go towards Medain Saleh, before the Baghdad Railway was planned, and cross over the Taurus Moun-

---

[206] L/P&S/10/12, "From Mr. G. Barclay to Sir Edward Grey (Confidential)," Istanbul, 17 November 1906 in *IOR*.

tains. The British interpreted the arrival of the Hejaz Railway in Medain Saleh, in 1907, as something to grapple with. British concerns over the Hejaz Railway were justified by the strong determination of Turkey to finish the project at all costs. Therefore, the British devised a policy of defying the real objectives of Pan-Islam[207].

---

207 L/P&S/10/12, "From Mr. G. Barclay to Sir Edward Grey (Confidential)," Istanbul, 17 November 1906 in *IOR*.

PART THREE

Stations, Geography, and Rail Lines

STATIONS, GEOGRAPHY, AND
RAIL LINES

ROUTES AND PORTS TO THE HEJAZ

The Hejaz had five loading ports: Yanbu or Yenbigh al-Bahr, Raies, Rabigh, Jeddah, and Lit. There were two major roads that served pilgrim caravans and military and commercial trafficking between Yanbu and Medina: Yanbu to al-Hamra through Missail and Bir al-Said, and Yanbu to al-Hait through the Adut al-Dunya and Adut al-Kuswa Mountains. The second road merged with the Mecca-Medina main road in Badr Kassa and it took five days to travel between Yanbu and Medina.

Two roads were located between Mecca and Jeddah. The first one was the main road that served the pilgrims and commercial activity. It consisted of twelve stages, each separated by a gendarmerie post, which stationed *Bishe*, the camelry, and *Hejinli*, the men on fast-moving Arabian camels called dromedaries, as guards. The second, also known as the Saidia Road, passed from Valley al-Barki through Rehra, Bahra Pess, Mikkat, Iranie, Valley, and Musifla all the way to Mecca.

There were four roads between Mecca and Medina and all of them, except for the eastern one passed, through Rabigh. The first one, called the Furaa road, reached the Valley Furaa though Rabigh. The second, known as the Ghair road, went to Aasa and Sata through Rabigh. The third, the *Sultanie*, or the Government Road, passed through Rabigh and reached Bir Mustawera, Bir Sheikh, Badr al-Saghira and Jedide. The fourth, the eastern road, went from Mecca to Medina through the Valley Limon, Mekrie, Masarabi al-Nefine, Sowerkie, and Hejrie. Lastly, Bir Sheikh, Badr al-Saghira, and Jedide were located on the road from Rabigh to Bir Mustawera and a road ran near Bir al-Sheikh between the Sultanie and the Ghair.

It was proposed that the Hejaz Railway follow the route that the pilgrims used between Mecca and Muzeirib. The following list gives travel times in hours to nearby settlements:

Mecca to the given location	Travel time in hours
Shedaiye	3
Valley Fatma	7
Osfan	13
Khalifa	8
Qadima	9
Rabigh	13

In addition, the list below gives the travel time in hours between cities, towns, and other settlements in the region:

Locations	Travel time in hours
Mecca to Mustawere Kapusi	10
Mecca to Sheikh Kapusi	12
Mecca to Bi'r al-Hisan	6
Mecca to Bi'r al-Kais	13
Mecca to Bi'r al-Ulema	14
Mecca to Medina	14
Medina to Bir Uthman (well)	1
Medina to Jebbur	10
Medina to Biar Nasia (wells)	10
Medina to Istabl Antera	14
Medina to Haidie	12
Medina to Bi'r Raiye	12
Medina to Bi'r-i Jeddid Qal'a	12
Medina to Zumurrud Qal'a	9
Medina to Biar al-Ghanema	12
Medain Saleh	10
Shuk al-Ajuz	12
Dar al-Hamra Qal'a	8
Al-Muazzam Qal'a	15
Al-Sani	9
Dar al-Ahther	8

Dar al-Maghura	10
Asie-Haremie Qal'a	8
Agh	11
Dar-el-Hajj Qal'a	11
Mudawwara	10
Aqaba-Al-Shamie	14,5
Ma'an	16,5
Aneize Qal'a	9
Al Hana	15
Qatrana	13
Bele Qal'a	11
Nehr al-Zurka Qal'a	16
Mefrik	8
Muzeirib	16

In Rabigh, a military post served as a place where pilgrims changed into their holy robes. From there, it took 24 hours by camel or five hours by train to reach Damascus; in other words, the total distance travelled between Mecca and Muzeirib was 1,398 miles or 437 hours.

GEOGRAPHICAL FEATURES OF THE REGION

The geography of the region along the line varied from stony and shallow valleys to desert areas, barely green with few shrubs or trees. The area between Ma'an and Medina presented 700 kilometers with such characteristics[208]. In southern Ma'an, there was the Arabia Petraea and for 38 miles in southern Ma'an there was a stony, undulating desert and several shallow valleys, which received little rainfall, once every two to three years. There were some shrubs and scattered acacia trees in these valleys. The rugged hills towards the Red Sea constituted the al-Hisme district, where several settlements were established near several small-sized springs and had mediocre vegetation. During the ancient Roman Empire, several small settlements existed there. In the immediate vicinity of the railroad, the terrain was more dull and straight. Aqaba Hejazie, not to be confused with Aqaba on the Red

---

[208] L/P&S/10/12, From Mr. G. Barclay to Sir Edward Grey (Confidential)," Istanbul, 17 November 1906 in *IOR*.

Sea, had a ruined *qal'a*, or castle, on the pilgrimage route, which had a cistern that could collect rainwater. To the south, there was the long escarpment of Batn al-Ghul, on which the railroad required a decline of nearly 500 feet. This wall of sandstone crags extended into a wide area to the northwest, and formed a similar obstruction across the Ma'an-Aqaba route. To the east, it extended for 40 miles that did not allow for easy passage, except for a narrow foot-path. The pilgrimage route found a fairly easy tumble alongside the railroad. In contrast to the brilliant red, yellow, and dazzling white of the rock and sand drifts, the black rocks, in twisted shapes and pinnacles, were eye-catching. The topography was unremarkable at the foot of the wide incline; an undulating plain of red sand and stones extended far south. The surface of the land presented many dark red or black pinnacles, which occasionally rose to flat-topped ridges.

To the west, there was a black-serrated ridge, swathed in drifts of sand for most of the way up until the slopes, and it formed a watershed with the Red Sea. Forty miles further to the east, there was a continuous scarp of red sandstone, which formed the edge of a plain in that direction.

The first permanent water source was a deep well in Mudawwara, 72 miles from Ma'an. Twenty miles to the south, after crossing the Haraat Ahmar, a ridge, recognizable by its many black pinnacles of rock and covered with drifts of sand and stones, led to Zat al-Hajj. Zat al-Hajj had an ancient stone-castle, half-a-dozen palm trees, and a reliable spring and well available at the station.

Jabal Sherora, the mountain also known as the "Pulpit of the Prophet", was striking with its slopes toward the region, rising in a circular pattern to a flat form with the top nearly 3,000 feet above the plain. Tabuk contained the first settlement after Ma'an: sixty houses of Negroid Arabs settled in an oasis of date palms and a few fruit gardens, which also had wheat fields, half a mile square, with water supply provided by a large spring. In fact, the station wells had a good supply of water and it was used to establish a large, local depot to support work in other regions to the south that did not have water.

Significantly, all the valleys from Batn al-Ghul in the north to Medain Saleh in the south disappeared in eastern Tabuk, at the foot of Jabal Sherora, and a season of extraordinarily heavy rain left a shallow lake there, which quickly dried up. Using artesian wells to counter the water shortages, was not considered until 1907.

In southern Tabuk, there was the Valley Ithil, or Valley Akhdar, through which the dry bed of the line passed on a stone bridge composed of twenty arches. Rain filled the valley only once every two or three years, but an unexpected rainstorm hit the valley in 1906. This made the construction of a bridge crucial, and there was six-foot high water flowing under it. Farther south no bridges were built. Considering the climate and rates of rainfall, the dry lands in that region did not require bridges; therefore no further funding was needed.

In nearby limestone hills, the terrain was more precarious. Prior to Akhdar, the railroad passed through a 180-meter tunnel to the Boghaz al-Akhdar, a rocky gorge, and then reached a narrow valley in the middle of steep, rocky hills, where the stone castle of Akhdar was located. There were no settlements in the region, but the castle had a functioning well with a constant supply of water. From here, the line followed the Valley Akhdar, a dry valley, from Disa'ad to Muazzam: the latter's stone castle provided a limited supply of water stored in cisterns for the pilgrims en route.

Muazzam was the closest point on the line to Teima. Medain Saleh's castle was built on rock-cut ruins with a well that had a poor supply of water, and the area's geography was not uniform. Before Medain Saleh, the railroad travelled through the Mabrak al-Naka, a rugged passage with limestone crags.

The lava-strewn plateau of Jabal Auered extended westward and shut off access to the sea; eastward, towards Teima and Hail, there were sandy plains crossed by a few rocky slopes. Teima was a fertile oasis in high open plains and an outbound colony from Jabal Shammar, with 250 houses, resided between palm groves. The railroad passed near the colony forty miles to the west; however, the location was important as it provided a route to Hail.

Thirty-five miles in southern Medain Saleh, the line reached the large oasis of al-Ula, the first settlement after Tabuk with a good water supply until Akhdar, nearly 150 miles to the north. It was planned to build another large depot on the line here, the last stop before Medina.

The region between Medain Saleh and Hadiyya, toward Medina, had more hills and far less water. However, a path was discovered following some of the smaller tributaries to the Valley Humd, and it provided a more manageable gradient. As the line advanced towards southern Al-Ula, the area was cut by an open valley, a tributary of the Valley Humd, which provided ease of passage to the line. The Valley Humd was the first location, amidst the hills that opened to the west, offering access to the Red Sea in Wej. This valley connected the region from Medina to Khyber, as well as the area around Al-Ula, and provided easy passage down to the coast.

Surrounded by lava formations and barren rocks, Khyber was another major oasis, though less fertile than Teima. The oasis was just off the line, approximately 40 miles in eastern Hadiyya. There were 4,000 inhabitants amidst abundant palm trees with several good springs. A busy route led to Hail, which made the oasis important. On the Red Sea, between Medina and Yanbu al-Bahr, there was another busy route, where a branch line between Medina and the coast could pass. From Medina to Mecca, the direction of the tracks had not been determined, nor were the preliminary surveys completed. The construction of the direct route, it was said, would be difficult and required passage through rough lands, as well as the territory of the Banu Harb. One of the construction proposals suggested removing the track east of the direct line, from Surveriye and Sefaine, down to the Valley Limon to Mecca. This route, however, would have no water supply, but would avoid the earlier, far rougher direction[209].

Another proposal suggested taking the track through Rabigh[210] to the coast and Mecca[211]. However, this would lengthen the distance of the line while saving the construction from severe engineering challenges and supplying it with water sources. In comparison, the eastern or highland route from Medina to Mecca would also save the construction from severe engineering challenges but would not provide the construction with a continuous source of water[212].

---

[209] L/P&S/10/12, "War Office to Foreign Office," 27 July 1907.

[210] Rabigh was a small town, with approximately 3,000 inhabitants, located three miles from the sea and 70 miles north of Jeddah. As a two-mile inlet, the town provided very good, wind-proof anchorage inside of eight to twelve fathoms and easy sailing backed by seasonal northwesterly winds. Eighteen to twenty fathoms was possible further in, with no bottom in a range of 30 fathoms. In addition, Rabigh was a holy town for Muslim pilgrims. It was in this town that the pilgrims coming over land from Medina to Mecca changed into special white garbs, the religious pilgrimage dress. L/P&S/10/12, "Sir N. O'Conor to Sir Edward Grey," Istanbul, 18 February 1908 in *IOR*.

[211] L/P&S/10/12, "War Office to Foreign Office," 27 July 1907 in *IOR*.

[212] L/P&S/10/12, "From Consul Monahan to Sir N. O'Conor," Jeddah, 3 February 1908 in *IOR*.

Main Rail Lines

The Hejaz Railroad Project was composed of two principal construction works, the main line and branch lines. While the main line extended between Damascus and Medina, the branch lines linked to the main line and previously constructed lines.

Damascus was the first station on the main line. From there, the main line continued to: Deraa, Amman, Jiza, Qatrana, Ma'an, Ghadr al-Haj, Batn al-Ghul, Mudawwara, Tabuk, Al-Akhdar, Al-Muazzam, Dar al-Hamra, Medain Saleh, Al-Ula, Hadiyya, and Medina.

Damascus–Medina Line

The distance between Damascus and Medina was approximately 1,500 miles[213]. The following are features of the stations on the way, given in the order of their distance, station name, ground level, details of the line, intermediate total: Damascus - Terminus + 696 feet.

A new terminus was established on the principal square, near the Government Serai. The line continued from Qadem past Maidan and Beramke, the stations of the French line that ran in parallel to the Hejaz line[214].

Distance from Qadem, Damascus-Qadem or Qadem al-Sharif

Damascus Station, or Qadem al-Sharif, was located in Barada, the provincial capital of Syria, with the military headquarters of the 5th Army Corps. Its population was approximately 180,000 and the garrison in the city held 12,000 soldiers. In total, approximately 150,000 residents were Muslims of Arab and Turkish origins. The rest included Christians and others: Orthodox Greeks, Greek Uniates, Armenians, Armenian Ministry, Syrian Ministry, Orthodox Syrians, Maronites, Roman Catholics, Protestants, and Chaldean Uniates, Jews, and Druzes[215]. This station was at the southern end of the long Maidan Quarter. It took half an hour of rough driving to reach the town center. It had a small station building, 33 by 12 yards (for goods) with a 63-yard platform. But, all the loading and un-

---

213 L/P&S/10/12, "W.S. Richards," Damascus, 8 February 1902.

214 L/P&S/10/12, "War Office to Foreign Office," 26 July 1907 in *IOR*.

215 L/P&S/10/12, From Mr. G. Barclay to Sir Edward Grey (Confidential)," Istanbul, 17 November 1906 in *IOR*.

loading took place in the open. It was an adequate station, especially for shipping, as the large-scale grain merchants in the region had their main offices and stores in the Maidan Quarter. Its sidings were 250 yards long. From there, the main road, 300 yards to the west, did not have any gates or enclosures. A branch line connected the French station of Maidan, half a mile to the northwest. In the east, parts of the Hejaz Railroad were under construction and repair shops were already operating. The construction and repair centers used electricity, provided by the Town Company plants[216], and had adequate water supplies[217].

Kiswe (2,425 feet)

Distance between the two stations: 20.8

Distance from the main station: 20.8

The Kiswe station had a siding of 250 yards. The station used the water source that was near the Kisror station[218], and there was a 25 cubic meter water tank and a steam pump[219]. A significant sized fellaheen village, with 1,200 inhabitants, stood on the Nahrel al-Wadi[220]. The large village of Kisror was across the Nahr Awadj Valley, one and a half miles to the northwest. The Muzeirib-Damascus road passed a mile to the west and a track connected it to the village. The French line passed a quarter mile from it. Khan Jenun, an old khan, which quartered a squadron of Nizam Cavalry, was on the road to the west. The line continued around the foot of Jabal Mania, turning to the east. Later, it passed Said Pasha's fertile farm that was irrigated by a canal from the Nahr Soil[221].

Dair Ali (2,287 feet)

Distance between the two stations: 9.8

Distance from the main station: 30.8

---

[216] L/P&S/10/12, "War Office to Foreign Office," 26 July 1907 in *IOR*.

[217] L/P&S/10/12, From Mr. G. Barclay to Sir Edward Grey (Confidential)," Istanbul, 17 November 1906 in *IOR*.

[218] L/P&S/10/12, From Mr. G. Barclay to Sir Edward Grey (Confidential)," Istanbul, 17 November 1906 in *IOR*.

[219] L/P&S/10/12, "War Office to Foreign Office," 26 July 1907 in *IOR*.

[220] L/P&S/10/12, From Mr. G. Barclay to Sir Edward Grey (Confidential)," Istanbul, 17 November 1906 in *IOR*.

[221] L/P&S/10/12, "War Office to Foreign Office," 26 July 1907 in *IOR*.

The Dair Ali station building had a 250 yard long siding[222]. The station was built on fertile terrain that provided spring water[223] and there was a 25 cubic meter water tank. In Dair Ali there was a Druze village. Approximately 500 Christian residents lived half a mile to the east. The line, there, inclined to the east over a cultivated plain[224].

Mismia 2,031 feet

Distance between the two stations: 20.9

Distance from the main station: 51.7

Mismia, or Mismia, was an Arab town built on ancient Roman ruins that covered two to three kilometers. Mismia served as a sanctuary to the brigand groups of the Leja. Mismia had a population of 700, composed of Muslims and Greek Orthodox[225]. Its station building was stone and had one siding. A mile to the south was a stone, two-storey barrack for one battalion, which was linked to the station by a good metalled road. The station stood on the edge of the Leja, a district covered with lava blocks, some 30 to 50 feet in depth, which provided refuge to all types of mobs and rebels. From there, Mismia commanded the northern exit. Some nearby springs provided sufficient water for the station, which had a 25 cubic meter water tank and pump. Several other springs watered the nearby meadows and supported grazing. The Hejaz railroad inclined here, to the west[226].

Jebab (2,110 feet)

Distance between the two stations: 11

Distance from the main station: 62.7

Jebab, a Muslim-Arab fellaheen village, hosted 300 residents[227]. Its station building was made of stone and had one siding on the edge of the Leja. The well did not offer the station a sufficient water supply[228].

222 L/P&S/10/12, "War Office to Foreign Office," 26 July 1907 in *IOR*.

223 L/P&S/10/12, From Mr. G. Barclay to Sir Edward Grey (Confidential)," Istanbul, 17 November 1906 in *IOR*.

224 L/P&S/10/12, "War Office to Foreign Office," 26 July 1907 in *IOR*.

225 L/P&S/10/12, From Mr. G. Barclay to Sir Edward Grey (Confidential)," Istanbul, 17 November 1906 in *IOR*.

226 L/P&S/10/12, "War Office to Foreign Office," 26 July 1907 in *IOR*.

227 L/P&S/10/12, From Mr. G. Barclay to Sir Edward Grey (Confidential)," Istanbul, 17 November 1906 in *IOR*.

228 L/P&S/10/12, "War Office to Foreign Office," 26 July 1907 in *IOR*.

Khebab (2,050 feet)

Distance between the two stations: 6.6

Distance from the main station: 69.3

Khebab was a Christian-Arab fellaheen village with approximately 600 residents[229]. Like the station in Jebab, the Khebab station had a well with a poor water supply. The line proceeded toward the edge of the Leja. In addition, several small villages in the region used the plain for cultivation to the west of the station[230].

Mehaye (1,975 feet)

Distance between the two stations: 8.7

Distance from the main station: 78

Mehaye, a Muslim-Arab fellaheen village, was an ancient Roman city, with 1,200 inhabitants[231]. The village had 50 stone houses on the east side. Its stone station building had one siding. The stone well supplied a fair amount of water, thanks to its 25 cubic-meter water tank. Just before the Ezra line, the railroad crossed a bridge between Valley Kanawat and Jabal Druz, where water flowed on a 30 foot-wide stony bed, but only in the spring. The bridge, also, had a 25-foot stone arch[232].

Shakra

Distance between the two stations: ---

Distance from the main station: ---

Shakra, a Muslim-Arab fellaheen village, was the site of an ancient Roman city and was inhabited by 800 residents, with several working wells[233].

Ezra (1,930 feet)

Distance between the two stations: 13.4

Distance from the main station: 91.4

---

[229] L/P&S/10/12, From Mr. G. Barclay to Sir Edward Grey (Confidential)," Istanbul, 17 November 1906 in *IOR*.

[230] L/P&S/10/12, "War Office to Foreign Office," 26 July 1907 in *IOR*.

[231] L/P&S/10/12, From Mr. G. Barclay to Sir Edward Grey (Confidential)," Istanbul, 17 November 1906 in *IOR*.

[232] L/P&S/10/12, "War Office to Foreign Office," 26 July 1907 in *IOR*.

[233] L/P&S/10/12, From Mr. G. Barclay to Sir Edward Grey (Confidential)," Istanbul, 17 November 1906 in *IOR*.

Ezra, ancient Boroa, bordered the Leja. It had a primarily Christian-Arab population, with 1,500 residents recorded shortly before the railroad construction reached the town. During the construction, the area was largely deserted when its inhabitants sought refuge from the Druzes. Its stone station building had one, 250-yard siding. The station gained greater significance in time, especially in exporting corn from the Hanran Plain and Jabal Druz. Occasionally, loads of corn waited a long time to be shipped. The border of the Leja was near the east end of Ezra, and a good metalled road crossed two miles to the south, leading from Sheikh Miskin to Bussorah and Jabal Druz. The station was in need of more sidings for its increasing volume of activity. A quarter mile before the Ghazala line, there was a crossing of a stony bed, 20 to 30 feet, from Jabal Druz. At the station, the steam pump and a 25 cubic-meter water tank did not offer much water[234]; however, there were three, well-maintained wells that served the old, local Christian churches and their followers[235].

Ghazala (1,889 feet)

Distance between the two stations: 14.9

Distance from the main station: 106.3

Ghazala, or Khirbit al-Ghazala, was a Muslim-Arab fellaheen village with 1,500 inhabitants[236]. The stone station building had one, 250-yard siding. It acted as an export hub for corn brought by camel caravans from the Hanran and Jabal Druz[237].

Deraa (1,735 feet)

Distance between the two stations: 16.9

Distance from the main station: 123.2

Deraa, ancient Edrée, had 400 houses and was on the far side of a deep ravine one mile to the southwest. Deraa was the seat of a *kaymakam*, i.e. a local governor, under the mutasarrıf of the Hauran in Sheikh Miskin[238]. It was a small town with 4,000 to 5,000 Muslim residents. The area had ruins with inscriptions that dated back to the Hellenistic (Necropolis) and Nabataic ages. An old

---

234 L/P&S/10/12, "War Office to Foreign Office," 26 July 1907 in *IOR*.
235 L/P&S/10/12, From Mr. G. Barclay to Sir Edward Grey (Confidential)," Istanbul, 17 November 1906 in *IOR*.
236 L/P&S/10/12, From Mr. G. Barclay to Sir Edward Grey (Confidential)," Istanbul, 17 November 1906 in *IOR*.
237 L/P&S/10/12, "War Office to Foreign Office," 26 July 1907 in *IOR*.
238 L/P&S/10/12, "War Office to Foreign Office," 26 July 1907 in *IOR*.

mosque also had cube inscriptions that dated back to the era of Omar the Caliph, which was restored by Sultan Salahuddin[239]. It had a large, two-storey, stone station building, an attached, covered cafeteria, and a 50-yard long platform. An adequate road facilitated access to the village. A portion of the corn trade from the Qauran ended up in this station. Four lines of sidings, 1,800 yards in total, were unable to handle the hectic traffic. Trains from all four directions intersected at noon, making one or two hour stops. The triangle was useful for the Haifa line in order to avoid turning the locomotive around[240]. In Deraa, there was an official, permanent traffic manager, and a section supervisor. To accommodate the officials, a decent-sized dwelling was used in Deraa[241]. There were two, 25 cubic-meter water tanks that pumped a sufficient quantity of water from the well. In addition, there was an engine shed for four engines, a repair shop for engines and carriages, and a coal-loading platform with a capacity of approximately 20 tons. A Greek-owned restaurant made of good quality stone, was built near the station, and provided food service that was demanded during the high season when an average of 50 to 60 tourists visited per day. The line climbed up to an open, cultivated area along the Valley Zedi and passed over a bridge, which stood on five, 20-foot stone arches. The bridge crossed over a stream that was 40 yards wide and one foot deep, on a rocky bed. There were 30-foot high piers. The stream did not flow in summer, and its bed was dry. It continued and crossed over two, 15-foot, stone, arched bridges over a smaller stream, which did not have a decent flow of water, even in the spring[242].

Nessib

Distance between the two stations: 12.7

Distance from the main station: 135.9

Nessib, a fellaheen village, located on a hill, had 150 houses and 700 residents and was one mile to the west side of the railroad. Its stone station building had one, 250-yard siding and cisterns[243]. The buildings were in better shape than those at the Damascus-Deraa section, where structures were lower, flat-

---

[239] L/P&S/10/12, From Mr. G. Barclay to Sir Edward Grey (Confidential)," Istanbul, 17 November 1906 in *IOR*.

[240] L/P&S/10/12, "War Office to Foreign Office," 26 July 1907 in *IOR*.

[241] L/P&S/10/12, From Mr. G. Barclay to Sir Edward Grey (Confidential)," Istanbul, 17 November 1906 in *IOR*.

[242] L/P&S/10/12, "War Office to Foreign Office," 26 July 1907 in *IOR*.

[243] L/P&S/10/12, From Mr. G. Barclay to Sir Edward Grey (Confidential)," Istanbul, 17 November 1906 in *IOR*.

roofed, and less accommodating. A few small culverts covered the stony ravines. It was a fertile country and was used for grazing during the spring[244].

Mafraq (1,961 feet)

Distance between the two stations: 25

Distance from the main station: 161.7

Mafraq, which was built on the ruins of an Arab Castle, Qal'at al-Mafraq, which was a Roman fortress on the Great Roman Road, Bostra Amman, had a large water reservoir made of stone[245]. A windmill pumped water to the station's water tank. It had three tunnels, a stone station building with a 250-yard siding, and a track of fertile lands without permanent residents, except for the Bedouins of the Banu Sakhr tribe that camped there. The pilgrimage route was on the west side.[246].

Samra (1,834 feet)

Distance between the two stations: 23.6

Distance from the main station: 185.3

Khirbet al-Samra was located above the ruins of a Roman castle on the Great Roman Road, Bostra Amman. The land was fertile and grazing was possible in the spring; and, 20,000 members of the Banu Sakhr tribe lived in 2,000 tents[247]. Its stone station building had one siding; and the railroad descended toward the Valley Zerqa, and crossed over the large Valley Dulgil and a stream, where water flowed in the spring[248].

Zerqa (2,027 feet)

Distance between the two stations: 47.4

Distance from the main station: 202.7

Zerqa, or Qal'at al-Zerqa, was on the Valley Zerqa, and had a continuous water supply. Qal'at al-Zerqa was a stone station building and had one siding on the edge of a plateau looking over the Valley Zerqa. There were

---

244 L/P&S/10/12, "War Office to Foreign Office," 26 July 1907 in *IOR*.
245 L/P&S/10/12, From Mr. G. Barclay to Sir Edward Grey (Confidential)," Istanbul, 17 November 1906 in *IOR*.
246 L/P&S/10/12, "War Office to Foreign Office," 26 July 1907 in *IOR*; L/P&S/10/12, From Mr. G. Barclay to Sir Edward Grey (Confidential)," Istanbul, 17 November 1906 in *IOR*.
247 L/P&S/10/12, "War Office to Foreign Office," 26 July 1907 in *IOR*; L/P&S/10/12, From Mr. G. Barclay to Sir Edward Grey (Confidential)," Istanbul, 17 November 1906 in *IOR*.
248 L/P&S/10/12, "War Office to Foreign Office," 26 July 1907 in *IOR*.

ruins of a Roman castle on the Great Roman Road, Bostra Amman. There was a Circassian village of 100 houses with refugees from Dagestan, Caucasus. It was located three-quarters of a mile to the west. Residents were composed of Circassians, the Banu Sakar family, and Bedouins[249]. Zerqa had rich, fertile lands and the valley was suitable for agriculture and irrigation was possible. Water came from a well or a 25 cubic-meter tank. In Zerqa, the line descended at a gradient of 1/62 to 1/55 into the Valley Zerqa, where there was a permanent stream and a tributary of the Jordan River.

Distance between the two stations: ---

Distance from the main station: 207

Here, the railroad crossed to the right bank with a stone bridge that had six, 20-foot arches and ascended along the valley at a gradient of 1/80[250].

Distance between the two stations: ---

Distance from the main station: 210

Here, the railroad crossed to the right bank with a stone bridge that was over 40 feet wide with six, 20-foot arches over a stream that had a stony bed. A few shrubs and low trees bordered the stream; and the valley was well cultivated[251].

Amman (2,418 feet)

Distance between the two stations: 19.7

Distance from the main station: 222.4

Located along the Nahr Amman, Amman, ancient Rabbath Ammon or Philadelphia, was the most significant and largest of the old towns of the East Jordan region. Mostly Circassians, with 700 to 800 houses, resided in the area. The ancient ruins, specifically the Greek theatre, thermae, and aerosols, were quite famous[252]. Its two-storey station building had a turntable, coal depot, and an engine-shed, where engines in use received maintenance and were repaired. The Amman station building had two, 300-yard sidings; and a store of rolling stock. Here, potable spring water served the station. From a 50 cubic-

---

[249] L/P&S/10/12, "From Mr. G. Barclay to Sir Edward Grey, (Confidential report by Auler Pasha on the Hejaz Railroad)," Istanbul, 17 November 1906 in *IOR*.

[250] L/P&S/10/12, "War Office to Foreign Office," 26 July 1907 in *IOR*.

[251] L/P&S/10/12, "War Office to Foreign Office," 26 July 1907 in *IOR*.

[252] L/P&S/10/12, From Mr. G. Barclay to Sir Edward Grey (Confidential)," Istanbul, 17 November 1906 in *IOR*.

meter tank, water was steam-pumped from a nearby river. The land in the area was extensively cultivated in the previous two years. In 1907, trains were only able to come to Kissir with five carriages; therefore, regular trains, excluding the duplex engines with greater power, could not pull all their carriages and were forced to run two trips. Here, the line went around the Amman Valley and climbed the southern heights towards a tributary ravine. There were sharp curves of 100 to 150 meter radii and increasing gradients of 1/55 and 1/45 in shorter sections. The sharpest curves of the entire railroad were in this region. In fact, several trains derailed in this region because of the high gradients[253].

Amman Viaduct
Distance between the two stations: ---
Distance from the main station: 232.2
The railroad crossed over a stone viaduct of ten arches with a span of 25 ft, and a supporting arch in the centre. The viaduct was 60 meters long and 20 meters high, and declined 40 feet and wound through rock cuttings and over an embankment of 60 ft. Then, the line passed though a dry ravine, with the main valley on the right[254].

Tunnel
Distance between the two stations: ---
Distance from the main station: ---
The line crossed over a valley, with a 20-foot stone bridge, and then passed around the head of another ravine through a 140-meter long, soft, white rock tunnel, on a curve with a 100-meter radius at a gradient of 1/45. Again, the line crossed over a ravine and passed through a rock cliff that was 40-feet deep. Thereafter, the line reached a wide-open area and hit the plateau's level after a few more rock cuttings[255].

Kassir (3,090 feet)
Distance between the two stations: 12.3
Distance from the main station: 234.5
Kassir, or Al-Sahl, contained the ruins of a Greek temple, or mausoleum. There was neither water nor residents, except for a few Bedouin tribes

---

253 L/P&S/10/12, "War Office to Foreign Office," 26 July 1907 in *IOR*.
254 L/P&S/10/12, "War Office to Foreign Office," 26 July 1907 in *IOR*.
255 L/P&S/10/12, "War Office to Foreign Office," 26 July 1907 in *IOR*.

who camped in winter[256]. The stone station building had one, 250-yard siding. Some cuttings, along the way, were made from white rock. It had tracks of fertile lands and grazing was possible in the spring. Later, the Circassian colony in Amman put the lands to good use. A steady, descending gradient rounded a wide loop for three kilometers of 1/70 to 1/80[257].

Libban (2,537 feet)

Distance between the two stations: 14.3

Distance from the main station: 248.8

Libban was located on the ruins of an ancient town built on two hills, near the adjoining ridge, and it had large cisterns. The stone station building, near the ruins, had a 250-yard siding. The remains of the ancient town were partially settled with 700 tents of the Bedouins of the Banu Sakhr tribe. Reimih ibn Fais, the sheikh of the tribe, lived in Libban, as well[258]. Water came from the cistern and the lands were semi-cultivated. In the spring, grazing was possible[259].

Jiza (2,385 feet)

Distance between the two stations: 10.9

Distance from the main station: 259.7

Jiza, or Qal'at al-Jiza, had several ruins of mostly Arab origin. Remarkably enough, the great Roman cisterns had a capacity of 70,000 cubic meters and there was a well-maintained old castle[260]. Its station building had a 250-yard siding. In addition to the cisterns, a 25 cubic-meter water tank and a windmill pump were used[261]. The fellaheen, from the Banu Sakhr tribe, inhabited Jiza[262]. The line passed through this undulating desert region and crossed two, wide valleys over stone bridges, with

---

[256] L/P&S/10/12, From Mr. G. Barclay to Sir Edward Grey (Confidential)," Istanbul, 17 November 1906 in *IOR*.

[257] L/P&S/10/12, "War Office to Foreign Office," 26 July 1907 in *IOR*.

[258] L/P&S/10/12, From Mr. G. Barclay to Sir Edward Grey (Confidential)," Istanbul, 17 November 1906 in *IOR*.

[259] L/P&S/10/12, "War Office to Foreign Office," 26 July 1907 in *IOR*.

[260] L/P&S/10/12, From Mr. G. Barclay to Sir Edward Grey (Confidential)," Istanbul, 17 November 1906 in *IOR*.

[261] L/P&S/10/12, "War Office to Foreign Office," 26 July 1907 in *IOR*.

[262] L/P&S/10/12, From Mr. G. Barclay to Sir Edward Grey (Confidential)," Istanbul, 17 November 1906 in *IOR*.

six, 20-foot arches. It had an ascending ratio of 1/55 to 1/50, and then sharply descended around a curve[263].

Deba'a

Distance between the two stations:---

Distance from the main station: 286

Deba'a, or Qal'at al-Deb'a, was an old castle restored in 1767 by Os-man Pasha, the leader of the Sacred Caravan. It was close to large cisterns and the Belka Bedouins, who were living in tents near the ruins, cultivated the land[264].

Delma (2,463 feet)

Distance between the two stations: 19

Distance from the main station: 278.7

The station building had one siding[265]. In Delma, there was a stone cas-tle and a large, rainwater cistern. Delma was an undulating, bare country with only minor cuttings. There were no sharp gradients. The station was near the pilgrimage route on the west side[266].

Khan Zebib (2,565 feet)

Distance between the two stations: 16.5

Distance from the main station: 275.2

Khan Zebib, or Hanesbib, was situated on the ruins of a large Arab car-avanserai, the flanking towers of the foundation suggest that it was used for defensive purposes. It was near a small Roman or Byzantine caravanserai and the remains of a Byzantine church. Numerous old cisterns in the area were not a source of water. Some Banu Sakhr Bedouins occasionally camped here[267]. Its station building had one siding. Khan Zebib had two viaducts made of six, 25-foot high, stone arches that crossed over a dry valley. The railroad passed undulating hills, rock, and clay cuttings for 11.8 miles and

---

263 L/P&S/10/12, "War Office to Foreign Office," 26 July 1907 in *IOR*.

264 L/P&S/10/12, From Mr. G. Barclay to Sir Edward Grey (Confidential)," Istanbul, 17 No-vember 1906 in *IOR*.

265 Siding was a secondary railroad track connected to the main track; wooden strips or some other material were used to cover the sides of buildings.

266 L/P&S/10/12, "War Office to Foreign Office," 26 July 1907 in *IOR*.

267 L/P&S/10/12, From Mr. G. Barclay to Sir Edward Grey (Confidential)," Istanbul, 17 No-vember 1906 in *IOR*.

then crossed over another bridge with six, 25-foot arches, which stood 30 feet above the ravine[268].

Siding

Distance between the two stations: 14.1

Distance from the main station: 309.3

Over a dry, rocky ravine, this siding had six, 25-foot arches, and the line ascended at 1/60. The local ravines led toward the Dead Sea in the west. Then, the line crossed a three to four mile-wide plain[269].

Qatrana

Distance between the two stations: 17.1

Distance from the main station: 326.4

In Qatrana, or Qal'at al-Qatrana, there was a Turkish castle on the pilgrimage route[270]. The railroad was located on the west side, and the castle had three cannons and two, 250-yard sidings. It was an administrative post. Similar to the Kerak station, which was six hours to the west, Qatrana was the government seat of the Mutasarrıf and had a one-battalion garrison. The station had a goods shed and a platform, 25 yards long and 3.5 feet high. Commercial activity was idle and water availability depended on the rain. In addition to the cannons, there was a large 70 x 50 yard reservoir that was stone-lined with cement, and had a capacity of 36,000 cubic meters. The windmill pumped into two, 25 cubic-meter water tanks[271]. The land was not suitable for cultivation. The Ibn al-Hedayn Bedouins camped here[272].

Siding

Distance between the two stations: 22

Distance from the main station: 348.4

There was a stone bridge with six, 25-foot arches right outside the station over the dry streambed, on which a dam was built to collect rain[273].

---

[268] L/P&S/10/12, "War Office to Foreign Office," 26 July 1907 in *IOR*.

[269] L/P&S/10/12, "War Office to Foreign Office," 26 July 1907 in *IOR*.

[270] L/P&S/10/12, From Mr. G. Barclay to Sir Edward Grey (Confidential)," Istanbul, 17 November 1906 in *IOR*.

[271] L/P&S/10/12, "War Office to Foreign Office," 26 July 1907 in *IOR*.

[272] L/P&S/10/12, From Mr. G. Barclay to Sir Edward Grey (Confidential)," Istanbul, 17 November 1906 in *IOR*.

[273] L/P&S/10/12, "War Office to Foreign Office," 26 July 1907 in *IOR*.

Siding

Distance between the two stations: 18.7

Distance from the main station: 367.1

The line took a steep ascent of 1/50 for a short distance and proceeded to an undulating terrain. Later, it followed a long descent of 1/55 into al-Hassa Valley, the head of the Valley Kerrahi, through two, deep rock cuttings[274].

Al-Hassa (3,696 feet)

Distance between the two stations: 10.7

Distance from the main station: 377.8

Al-Hassa, or Qal'at al-Hassa, had a large, two-storey castle that was built by Sultan Mustafa, around 1760, which had been partly destroyed. There was a spring inside, on the east side of the castle. An 80-foot well in the courtyard supplied water into an ancient cistern[275]. The station had an adequate supply of water from the well[276]. The station building in Al-Hassa had a 250-yard siding. The line crossed a dry valley bed over a stone bridge of three, 25-foot arches and ascended at a rate of 1/66 towards the end of the valley, passed over a tributary ravine, and through a stony plain strewn with black pebbles of obsidian. Few vegetables grew,[277] but the land was fertile[278].

Jerouf al-Darawish (3,220 feet)

Distance between the two stations: 19.6

Distance from the main station: 397.4

In addition to a station building and one siding of 250 yards,[279] Jerouf al-Darawish had an old Roman castle that was 36 square meters in area with 1.70-meter thick walls, and was on the pilgrimage route. On the southeast side, there was a large watchtower[280]. No source of water was available. The line ascended a long gradient of 1/80 after the station and skirted a deep ra-

---

274 L/P&S/10/12, "War Office to Foreign Office," 26 July 1907 in *IOR*.

275 L/P&S/10/12, "War Office to Foreign Office," 26 July 1907 in *IOR*.

276 L/P&S/10/12, From Mr. G. Barclay to Sir Edward Grey (Confidential)," Istanbul, 17 November 1906 in *IOR*.

277 L/P&S/10/12, "War Office to Foreign Office," 26 July 1907 in *IOR*.

278 L/P&S/10/12, "From Mr. G. Barclay to Sir Edward Grey (Confidential)," Istanbul, 17 November 1906 in *IOR*.

279 L/P&S/10/12, "War Office to Foreign Office," 26 July 1907 in *IOR*.

280 L/P&S/10/12, "From Mr. G. Barclay to Sir Edward Grey (Confidential)," Istanbul, 17 November 1906 in *IOR*.

vine along a stony, undulating, and uncultivated plain. A flat-topped range of hills continued approximately three miles to the east[281]. Nearly 160 Bedouins settled in this area and the Anweitat Bedouins visited the wells[282].

Uneiza (3,448 feet)

Distance between the two stations: 25.2

Distance from the main station: 422.6

Uneiza, or Qal'at Uneiza, had a modern Turkish castle near damaged rain cisterns[283] on the pilgrimage route. Its station building had one, 250-yard siding[284]. On the northwest side there was Sa'djunije, the Roman castle, with a 100-meter square foundation. Three kilometers from the station stood Al-Halla, a dormant volcano, with a clearly visible crater. The land was fertile in Uneiza, but lacked a water source. The Huweitat Bedouins were the inhabitants of the region and they lived in tents[285].

Siding

Distance between the two stations: 440.5

Distance from the main station: 18.3

In this area, there was no water supply[286].

Ma'an (3,540 feet)

Distance between the two stations:---

Distance from the main station: 459.14

As well as its extensive sidings, the Ma'an station had a significantly sized depot and an engine shed, turntable, coaling depot, repair shop, and small goods shed. The construction offices for the line to the south were also located here. [287]. Ma'an, an oasis in the desert, hosted Ma'an al-Shamie

---

281 L/P&S/10/12, "War Office to Foreign Office," 26 July 1907 in *IOR*.

282 L/P&S/10/12, "From Mr. G. Barclay to Sir Edward Grey (Confidential)," Istanbul, 17 November 1906 in *IOR*.

283 L/P&S/10/12, "From Mr. G. Barclay to Sir Edward Grey (Confidential)," Istanbul, 17 November 1906 in *IOR*.

284 L/P&S/10/12, "War Office to Foreign Office," 26 July 1907 in *IOR*.

285 L/P&S/10/12, "From Mr. G. Barclay to Sir Edward Grey (Confidential)," Istanbul, 17 November 1906 in *IOR*.

286 L/P&S/10/12, "From Mr. G. Barclay to Sir Edward Grey (Confidential)," Istanbul, 17 November 1906 in *IOR*.

287 L/P&S/10/12, "War Office to Foreign Office," 26 July 1907 in *IOR*.

and Ma'an-Misrie, two villages approximately one kilometer apart[288]. The former contained approximately 200 houses and was two kilometers to the south of the station. A Roman castle stood there; and water was abundant. Ma'an-Misrie, the latter village, had 500 houses; and an adequate amount of water supplied from the springs in limestone helped to irrigate gardens and supported cultivation[289]. Ma'an had small clay huts, narrow valleys, plenty of spring water,[290] and good quality water supplied from wells:[291] as well as palms, figs, and pomegranates. Furthermore, the residents of the village earned their living from visiting pilgrims[292]. Ma'an was the seat of the Kaymakam, the local governor, and had a military garrison of two companies and a supply depot for the posts on the Aqaba route. Later, a military hospital with 100 beds was built near the station. Towards the east, in the Hisme hills, there were a number of settled Arab communities and several small springs. To the southwest, the area lacked water and remained largely uninhabited.[293] When the main line reached Ma'an in 1904, preparations began for the construction of the branch line to the Gulf of Aqaba. A year later, the station and other buildings were built to serve the junction[294].

Distance between the two stations: 475.0

Distance from the main station: 12.0

The siding was built, but no water was available[295].

Distance between the two stations: 4878.0

Distance from the main station: 12.0

There was a siding but no water [296].

---

[288] L/P&S/10/12, "From Mr. G. Barclay to Sir Edward Grey (Confidential)," Istanbul, 17 November 1906 in *IOR*.

[289] L/P&S/10/12, "War Office to Foreign Office," 26 July 1907 in *IOR*.

[290] L/P&S/10/12, "From Mr. G. Barclay to Sir Edward Grey (Confidential)," Istanbul, 17 November 1906 in *IOR*.

[291] L/P&S/10/12, "War Office to Foreign Office," 26 July 1907 in *IOR*.

[292] L/P&S/10/12, "From Mr. G. Barclay to Sir Edward Grey (Confidential)," Istanbul, 17 November 1906 in *IOR*.

[293] L/P&S/10/12, "War Office to Foreign Office," 26 July 1907 in *IOR*.

[294] L/P&S/10/12, "From Sir N. O'Conor to Sir Edward Grey (Confidential)," Istanbul, 12 June 1906 in *IOR*.

[295] L/P&S/10/12, "From Mr. G. Barclay to Sir Edward Grey (Confidential)," Istanbul, 17 November 1906 in *IOR*.

[296] L/P&S/10/12, "From Mr. G. Barclay to Sir Edward Grey (Confidential)," Istanbul, 17 November 1906 in *IOR*.

Ghadr al-Haj (3,270 feet)

Distance between the two stations: 15.86

Distance from the main station: 475.10

In Ghadr al-Haj, the station and other buildings were established, as well as two tents. The station building had one, 250-yard siding. In absence of a natural source of water, only a few trees and shrubs grew. The area, in general, looked like a stony and waterless desert with some small valleys. The pilgrimage route ran parallel to the railroad[297].

Bir Shedia

Distance between the two stations: 12.15

Distance from the main station: 487.15

In Bir Shedia, there was only one stone station building with one siding and ten officials. There were several small valleys in the region, but there was no natural source of water and only seven water barrels sunk into the ground[298].

Guard House

Distance between the two stations: ---

Distance from the main station: 495

The Guard House was a simple, stone building with no siding. Water was supplied with barrels[299].

Guard House

Distance between the two stations: ---

Distance from the main station: 501

Similar to the preceding Guard House, water was supplied with barrels. The establishment had no siding, but had two guard tents[300].

Bridge

Distance between the two stations: ---

Distance from the main station: 506

---

[297] L/P&S/10/12, "War Office to Foreign Office," 26 July 1907 in *IOR*.

[298] L/P&S/10/12, "War Office to Foreign Office," 26 July 1907 in *IOR*.

[299] L/P&S/10/12, "War Office to Foreign Office," 26 July 1907 in *IOR*.

[300] L/P&S/10/12, "War Office to Foreign Office," 26 July 1907 in *IOR*.

The line crossed over a large valley by a bridge that was supported by six, 20-foot stone arches[301].

Guard House

Distance between the two stations: ---

Distance from the main station: 507

This Guard House had two guard tents and water was supplied with barrels. It had no siding. Thirty to forty miles to the east, a sharp line of hills was visible. The area was a stony desert; only a few low trees and shrubs grew in the valley[302].

Aqaba (3,630 feet)

Distance between the two stations: 26.35

Distance from the main station: 514.50

Aqaba, also known as Aqaba Hejazie to distinguish it from the Aqaba on the Red Sea, and was known as Aqaba Misrie on the pilgrimage route[303]. Aqaba Hejazie was a pilgrimage route, 2.5 kilometers away from the pilgrimage caravan station of the same name[304].

Aqaba had two stone station buildings in addition to an ancient castle. The buildings had one, 260-yard siding and cisterns with a capacity of approximately 12,000 cubic meters. The Bedouins of Huweitat camped here. Several other tracks over the desert paralleled the Hejaz railroad. The Hejaz line climbed to a broad col on the skirt of a valley, which was neighbored by a few shrubs, and, after a stony ravine, sharply descended[305].

Batn al-Ghul (3,710 feet)

Distance between the two stations: 6

Distance from the main station: 520.50

---

301 L/P&S/10/12, "War Office to Foreign Office," 26 July 1907 in *IOR*.
302 L/P&S/10/12, "War Office to Foreign Office," 26 July 1907 in *IOR*.
303 L/P&S/10/12, "From Mr. G. Barclay to Sir Edward Grey (Confidential)," Istanbul, 17 November 1906 in *IOR*; L/P&S/10/12, "War Office to Foreign Office," 26 July 1907 in *IOR*.
304 L/P&S/10/12, "From Mr. G. Barclay to Sir Edward Grey (Confidential)," Istanbul, 17 November 1906 in *IOR*.
305 L/P&S/10/12, "War Office to Foreign Office," 26 July 1907 in *IOR*.

At Batn al-Ghul, i.e. the Monster's Belly, the line sharply descended from the mountainside[306]. Its station building was composed of one siding and two stone houses. In absence of a natural source of water, six barrels sunk into the ground provided water. Batn al-Ghul was on the edge of a short cliff with a series of relaxed slopes, which descended down the pilgrimage route. Wheeled transportation was possible. Approximately 30 miles to the east and further to the west, there was no other practical way to pass the cliff, a line of lime-stone and sandstones of 300 to 400 feet, with a 500-foot decline. The railroad curved sharply after leaving the station and descended in parallel to the hillside with a wide loop towards the west. Specifically, the rolling gradient was 18/1,000. Another sharp curve followed at the end of the loop. There was no bridge, but a number of small stone culverts[307]. The landscape of the region was magnificent because of the broken sandstone mountains of remarkable and various colors[308].

   ---   524   ---

This section was located at the foot of the main decline. The line followed a two-mile wide valley that was bordered by remarkably shaped black rocks to the west, and lime and sand stones to the east. The bed of the valley, called the Valley Rutm, had sand drifts and stones [309].

Siding

Distance between the two stations: 15.0

Distance from the main station: 530.0

There was a walled reservoir and the water was brought by water carrying trains in order to provide passing trains[310].

Valley Rutm (3,215 feet)

Distance between the two stations: 9.65

Distance from the main station: 530.15

---

[306] L/P&S/10/12, "From Mr. G. Barclay to Sir Edward Grey (Confidential)," Istanbul, 17 November 1906 in *IOR*.

[307] L/P&S/10/12, "War Office to Foreign Office," 26 July 1907 in *IOR*.

[308] L/P&S/10/12, "From Mr. G. Barclay to Sir Edward Grey (Confidential)," Istanbul, 17 November 1906 in *IOR*.

[309] L/P&S/10/12, "War Office to Foreign Office," 26 July 1907 in *IOR*.

[310] L/P&S/10/12, "From Mr. G. Barclay to Sir Edward Grey (Confidential)," Istanbul, 17 November 1906 in *IOR*.

In the Valley Rutm, the station complex was composed of one siding and two stone houses. There was an unused, stone water tank. In absence of a natural source of water, six barrels were sunk into the ground.

533   ---   ---

A valley was located here. The line passed though a stony desert with drift sands. Isolated rocky pinnacles emerged in the west, approximately 30 miles later there was a coastal range, a very rugged line of hills with sharply defined summits, and various crags and pinnacles. There was a panoramic view in the southeast over a plain, with several isolated ridges. The pilgrimage route and telegraph line ran in parallel with the railroad on the west side[311].

Siding

Distance between the two stations: 9.0

Distance from the main station: 545.0

This location had a lack of water[312].

Tel Shahm (2,770 feet)

Distance between the two stations: 16.41

Distance from the main station: 546.56

Tel Shahm had a station building with one siding. In absence of a natural source of water, six barrels were sunk into the ground. The low rugged hills, two miles further in the west, had a magnificent landscape.

Siding

Distance between the two stations: 18.0

Distance from the main station: 554.0

This location had a lack of water [313].

Ramle (2,625 feet)

Distance between the two stations: 9.84

Distance from the main station: 555.40

---

[311] L/P&S/10/12, "War Office to Foreign Office," 26 July 1907 in *IOR*.

[312] L/P&S/10/12, "From Mr. G. Barclay to Sir Edward Grey (Confidential)," Istanbul, 17 November 1906 in *IOR*.

[313] L/P&S/10/12, "From Mr. G. Barclay to Sir Edward Grey (Confidential)," Istanbul, 17 November 1906 in *IOR*.

Ramle had a station building with one siding. In absence of a natural source of water, six barrels were sunk into the ground[314].

Qal'a al-Mudawwara (2,345 feet)

Distance between the two stations: 16.90

Distance from the main station: 572.30

Qal'at-i Mudawwara, or Mudawwara Station, was 3.5 kilometers from Qal'at and 72 miles from Ma'an. Qal'at-i Mudawwara had a permanent source of water, but the source, a deep well, did not offer an adequate supply of water[315]. The old Qal'a was located among the rocky hills eight miles further west, not visible from the station. The well functioned moderately well and the pilgrimage route and telegraph line passed though there. The station complex had two stone buildings with two, 200-yard sidings. It was not a favorable station due to its poor water supply. The only source of water was the wells: an 80-foot deep well was used with a windmill pump, but the water provided was not abundant. In addition, there were two galvanized, 50 cubic-meter iron tanks on a stone tower. The engine shed, which could serve two engines simultaneously, was not in active service[316]. The Bedouins, especially those who frequented Qal'at-i Mudawwara, were from the Huweitat tribe, from the mountains on the west side. The Banu Atie Bedouins also camped here[317].

Guard Post

Distance between the two stations: ---

Distance from the main station: ---

At this guard post, there were two tents with three grounded barrels to supply water and one siding.

Haraat Ahmar (2,480 feet)

Distance between the two stations: 22.57

Distance from the main station: 594.87

---

314 L/P&S/10/12, "War Office to Foreign Office," 26 July 1907 in *IOR*.

315 L/P&S/10/12, "From Mr. G. Barclay to Sir Edward Grey (Confidential)," Istanbul, 17 November 1906 in *IOR*.

316 L/P&S/10/12, "War Office to Foreign Office," 26 July 1907 in *IOR*.

317 L/P&S/10/12, "From Mr. G. Barclay to Sir Edward Grey (Confidential)," Istanbul, 17 November 1906 in *IOR*.

Haraat Ahmar had a station building with one siding. In absence of a natural source of water, six barrels were sunk into the ground[318].

Guard Post

Distance between the two stations: ---

Distance from the main station: ---

At this guard post, there were two tents with four, grounded barrels to supply water and one siding[319].

Zat al-Hajj (2,315 feet)

Distance between the two stations: 13.80

Distance from the main station: 608.67

Zat al-Hajj was an area defined by many black rock pinnacles and covered with sand drifts and stones. The area included an ancient stone castle, half-a-dozen palm trees, one good spring, and a well at the station complex[320]. The station complex had two, single-sided station buildings. It was a quarter of a mile west from the ancient stone fort on the pilgrimage route. Water was plentiful and there were pools between the station and Qal'a, the fort. Six gendarmeries guarded the Qal'a[321]. Bedouin tribes inhabited Zat al-Hajj; specifically, the Banu Artéje tribe lived there in 200 tents[322].

Bir ibn Hermas (2,425 feet)

Distance between the two stations: 0.60

Distance from the main station: 632.27

Bir ibn Hermas had a station building with one siding. Water came from a well, but it was not as abundant as the well in Zat al-Hajj. Three to four feet deep, two tanks had a capacity of 25 cubic meters and were supported by windmill pumps[323].

---

[318] L/P&S/10/12, "War Office to Foreign Office," 26 July 1907 in *IOR*.

[319] L/P&S/10/12, "War Office to Foreign Office," 26 July 1907 in *IOR*.

[320] L/P&S/10/12, "From Mr. G. Barclay to Sir Edward Grey (Confidential)," Istanbul, 17 November 1906 in *IOR*.

[321] L/P&S/10/12, "War Office to Foreign Office," 26 July 1907 in *IOR*.

[322] L/P&S/10/12, "From Mr. G. Barclay to Sir Edward Grey (Confidential)," Istanbul, 17 November 1906 in *IOR*.

[323] L/P&S/10/12, "War Office to Foreign Office," 26 July 1907 in *IOR*.

Al-Hazm (2,200 feet)

Distance between the two stations: 22.50

Distance from the main station: 654.77

Al-Hazm had a single-sided station building, with no natural source of water. A wide basin extended to Jabal Sherora to the east, with a remarkable peak bearing 68 degrees approximately 40 miles later. A very rugged ridge stood to the west that paralleled the coast[324].

Muhtahab (2,395 feet)

Distance between the two stations: 23.13

Distance from the main station: 677.90

Muhtahab had a single-sided station building with a well that did not provide an adequate supply of salty water[325].

Tabuk (2,560 feet)

Distance between the two stations: 24.38

Distance from the main station: 692.28

The city of Tabuk was located approximately 190 kilometers from Ma'an[326]. In Tabuk, there was an ancient castle with small palm groves, about 1,000 date trees, a few fruit gardens, and wheat fields, which covered an area of approximately half a mile, and were watered from a large spring. The Banu Artéje collected the fruit and brought it to Ma'an once a year. Tabuk was the first settlement after Ma'an, with 60 houses of the Black Arabs, who lived in an oasis of date trees. Twenty-five Bedouin families lived in the houses[327]. Near the castle, one mile further to the west of the station[328], there was a village located in the middle of date trees in Tabuk. Although the village was in ruins and uninhabited, it came under construction after the building of the railroad started. The station wells, 12-feet below the ground, supplied a good amount of water, and officials took advantage of channeling this source of water into large, 25 cubic-meter water depots with

---

324 L/P&S/10/12, "War Office to Foreign Office," 26 July 1907 in *IOR*.

325 L/P&S/10/12, "War Office to Foreign Office," 26 July 1907 in *IOR*.

326 L/P&S/10/12, "From Mr. G. Barclay to Sir Edward Grey (Confidential)," Istanbul, 17 November 1906 in *IOR*.

327 L/P&S/10/12, "From Mr. G. Barclay to Sir Edward Grey, (Confidential report by Auler Pasha on the Hejaz Railroad)," Istanbul, 17 November 1906 in *IOR*.

328 L/P&S/10/12, "War Office to Foreign Office," 26 July 1907 in *IOR*.

the help of windmill pumps, in an effort to advance the construction farther to the south, where there was a lack of water[329]. During the course of completing the station, it was planned to include an engine shed, repair shop, turntable, and general depot.

Valley Ithil (2,821 feet)

Distance between the two stations: ---

Distance from the main station: 721

Valley Ithil, or Al-Til, had one fortified station building with no natural source of water[330].

Dar al-Haj (3,050 feet)

Distance between the two stations: 24

Distance from the main station: 745

Dar al-Haj had a single-sided and fortified station building with no supply of water. A limestone spur required the line to pass through a 180-meter tunnel and then passed a small, open basin[331].

Mustabgha (3,115 feet)

Distance between the two stations: 11

Distance from the main station: 756

Mustabgha had a single sided, fortified station building with no natural supply of water. The narrow gorge in the sandstone hills, leading down to Qal'at-i Akhdar, was called the Boghaz al-Akhdar[332].

Qal'at al-Akhdar (2,920 feet)

Distance between the two stations: 5

Distance from the main station: 761

Qal'at al-Akhdar, or Al-Khuthr as the local nomads called it[333], was a narrow valley between steep, rocky hills where the stone castle of Akhdar was located, with sandstone bridges on both sides of the pilgrimage road. Qal'at al-Akhdar had one, fortified station building. The area was known for having the

---

[329] L/P&S/10/12, "From Mr. G. Barclay to Sir Edward Grey (Confidential)," Istanbul, 17 November 1906 in *IOR*.

[330] L/P&S/10/12, "War Office to Foreign Office," 26 July 1907 in *IOR*.

[331] L/P&S/10/12, "War Office to Foreign Office," 26 July 1907 in *IOR*.

[332] L/P&S/10/12, "War Office to Foreign Office," 26 July 1907 in *IOR*.

[333] L/P&S/10/12, "War Office to Foreign Office," 26 July 1907 in *IOR*.

highest quality of water on the pilgrimage route. Water came from an excellent, shallow well that served as a constant supply of water, available inside the castle[334]. From inside the well, a noria wheel, turned by mules, carried the water into the cisterns, three in front and three further in the west[335]. There was not a significant number of trees or bushes; and because the desert ground was not suitable for cultivation, there were no settlements. Approximately 70 members of the Banu Artéje tribe lived there, in tents[336].

Khamis (3,035 feet)

Distance between the two stations: 22

Distance from the main station: 783

Khamis had a station building as the Valley Sani with no water available. There were a few acacia trees in the valley.

Disa'ad (3,100 feet)

Distance between the two stations: 23

Distance from the main station: 806

Disa'ad had one station building at the north end of the Valley Sani. There were some acacia trees and bushes in the dry bed of the valley, but no water was available[337].

Muazzam (3,250 feet)

Distance between the two stations: 23

Distance from the main station: 829

In Al-Muazzam there was a Qal'a, castle, located on the pilgrimage route. The castle had a large *birket*, cistern, to accumulate rainwater. The ancient reservoir in Al-Muazzam had a capacity of 11,000 cubic meters. However, after it was cleaned and repaired, the reservoir increased its capacity to 16,000 cubic meters[338]. The Fejir and Khuthera families of the Banu Atie

---

334 L/P&S/10/12, "War Office to Foreign Office, (Report of the Major Maunsell, R.A. on the H.R.)," 27 July 1907 in *IOR*.

335 L/P&S/10/12, "War Office to Foreign Office," 26 July 1907 in *IOR*.

336 L/P&S/10/12, "From Mr. G. Barclay to Sir Edward Grey (Confidential)," Istanbul, 17 November 1906 in *IOR*.

337 L/P&S/10/12, "From Mr. G. Barclay to Sir Edward Grey (Confidential)," Istanbul, 17 November 1906 in *IOR*.

338 L/P&S/10/12, "Sir N. O'Conor to Sir Edward Grey," Istanbul, 25 September 1907 in *IOR*.

tribe traveled within the region[339]. In addition, 100 members of the Abu Shama tribe lived here[340].

Khat al-Zane (3,480 feet)

Distance between the two stations: 26

Distance from the main station: 854

The station in Khat al-Zane was located in a sandy valley between cliffs with no water supply[341].

Dar al-Hamra (3,710 feet)

Distance between the two stations: 27

Distance from the main station: 881

In Dar al-Hamra, there were ruins of a Qal'a, or castle, on the pilgrimage road. There was, also, a birket, or cistern, in the valley's bed, which was filled by rainfall in the winter. The valley was dry most of the time and in bad condition[342]. One hundred and fifty Bedouins of the Abu Shama tribe lived in the region[343].

Al-Mutalli (3,640 feet)

Distance between the two stations: 24

Distance from the main station: 905

Al-Mutalli had sandstone crags and a deep, sandy landscape. Through the Shuk al-Ajuz, there was a passage in the rough sandstone ridges. The area lacked a reliable water source[344].

Abu Taqa (3,150 feet)

Distance between the two stations: 14

Distance from the main station: 919

---

[339] L/P&S/10/12, "From Mr. G. Barclay to Sir Edward Grey (Confidential)," Istanbul, 17 November 1906 in *IOR*; L/P&S/10/12, "War Office to Foreign Office," 26 July 1907 in *IOR*.

[340] L/P&S/10/12, "From Mr. G. Barclay to Sir Edward Grey (Confidential)," Istanbul, 17 November 1906 in *IOR*.

[341] L/P&S/10/12, "War Office to Foreign Office," 26 July 1907 in *IOR*.

[342] L/P&S/10/12, "War Office to Foreign Office," 26 July 1907 in *IOR*.

[343] L/P&S/10/12, "From Mr. G. Barclay to Sir Edward Grey (Confidential)," Istanbul, 17 November 1906 in *IOR*.

[344] L/P&S/10/12, "War Office to Foreign Office," 26 July 1907 in *IOR*.

The Abu Taqa station was located in an area with sandstone crags and did not have a supply of water[345].

Al-Mazham (2,985 feet)

Distance between the two stations: 14

Distance from the main station: 931

Al-Mazham had a narrow passage between sandstone hills around the western side of the Mabrak al-Naka, a steep, sandstone ridge. Water was not available and there were only a few acacia trees and bushes scattered in the area. The line descended into the plain, Medain Saleh [346].

Medain Saleh (2,600 feet)

Distance between the two stations: 24

Distance from the main station: 955

Medain Saleh, known as the birthplace of the Prophet Saleh, was built on the ruins of Hedjr. In Jewish tradition, the town was the old Egra of Ptolemy, an ancient Jewish capital. In Medain Saleh, there was a castle among rock cliffs on the pilgrimage route. In the courtyard, there was the working, 26-foot deep, Bir al-Naga well. Spring water was not available[347]. An 18 to 22-yard cistern in the south was filled with water from the well with the help of a noria wheel that was turned by two mules. In fact, water was poor in quality and quantity[348]. Medain Saleh was ideal for a military base, which could operate in Central Arabia and the Nejd[349]. Al-Fajir and Beda Bedouins lived here in 300 tents[350].

Al-Ula (2,035 feet)

Distance between the two stations: ---

Distance from the main station: 1,015

---

345 L/P&S/10/12, "War Office to Foreign Office," 26 July 1907 in *IOR*.

346 L/P&S/10/12, "War Office to Foreign Office," 26 July 1907 in *IOR*.

347 L/P&S/10/12, "From Mr. G. Barclay to Sir Edward Grey (Confidential)," Istanbul, 17 November 1906 in *IOR*.

348 L/P&S/10/12, "War Office to Foreign Office," 26 July 1907 in *IOR*.

349 L/P&S/10/12, "From Mr. G. Barclay to Sir Edward Grey (Confidential)," Istanbul, 17 November 1906 in *IOR*.

350 L/P&S/10/12, "War Office to Foreign Office," 26 July 1907 in *IOR*; L/P&S/10/12, "From Mr. G. Barclay to Sir Edward Grey (Confidential)," Istanbul, 17 November 1906 in *IOR*.

Al-Ula, the first settlement after Tabuk with approximately 400 houses and 2,000 inhabitants, was situated at an oasis of date palms, which was approximately two miles long. The area had a good source of water after Akhdar, approximately 150 miles further north[351]. Al-Ula was a small town that was surrounded by defensive walls. The town had two main gates and stood against the sharp cliff of the Harra. Corn could grow and dates were plenty. Water was of good quantity and available from a series of slightly warm springs in the Valley al-Kurra. A small stream was used for watering the gardens. A small number of cattle, donkeys, goats, and poultry were available[352]. As in Ma'an and Tabuk, a railroad depot was built here[353]. A line track led towards Al-Wej, on the Red Sea[354].

Qal'a Zumurrud (2,165 feet)

Distance between the two stations: ---

Distance from the main station: 1,030

Qal'a Zumurrud was located in a narrow, rocky canyon on the pilgrimage route. Its cisterns provided water[355].

Hadiyya (1,250 feet)

Distance between the two stations: ---

Distance from the main station: 1,135

Hadiyya was on the pilgrimage route and provided a fair source of water from its wells. It took one day to walk from Hadiyya to Khyber[356]."

Medina (1,320 feet)

Distance between the two stations: ---

Distance from the main station: 1,300.

---

[351] L/P&S/10/12, "War Office to Foreign Office," 26 July 1907 in *IOR*; L/P&S/10/12, "From Mr. G. Barclay to Sir Edward Grey (Confidential)," Istanbul, 17 November 1906 in *IOR*.

[352] L/P&S/10/12, "War Office to Foreign Office," 26 July 1907 in *IOR*.

[353] L/P&S/10/12, "From Mr. G. Barclay to Sir Edward Grey (Confidential)," Istanbul, 17 November 1906 in *IOR*.

[354] L/P&S/10/12, "War Office to Foreign Office," 26 July 1907 in *IOR*.

[355] L/P&S/10/12, "War Office to Foreign Office," 26 July 1907 in *IOR*.

[356] L/P&S/10/12, "War Office to Foreign Office," 26 July 1907 in *IOR*.

SUB-LINES

The priority of the Hejaz Railway was to complete the line, as soon as possible, up to Medina, the first of the Holy Cities. As a result, all efforts focused on the construction. It was hoped that the line would reach Medina by September 1908. According to the project's plan, the construction would not continue towards Mecca and, instead, focus would shift to the construction of a sheltered port in Haifa, with the Jeddah-Mecca section to be used by the Indian pilgrims, and some branch lines in Syria to generate revenue. It was only after the completion of these plans that construction would begin on the Medina-Mecca line, as well as the following branch lines: Amman-Salt, Haifa-Acre branch, Afule-Nablus-Jerusalem, and Tel al-Shemmam-Plain of Sharon-Jaffa[357].

The construction commission intended to construct these branch lines; however, the British did not approve of the construction of the branch lines to al-Salt and of the line between Amman and Jerusalem, simply because these constructions would have shortcomings[358].

AMMAN—AL-SALT

The Amman-Al-Salt branch line, 38 kilometers, was intended to help utilize the phosphate deposits between the stations, which were conferred to the Hejaz Railroad's construction. This branch would be the starting point of a line to connect the Hejaz Railroad and the English Jaffa-Jerusalem line, and would lead down to the coast. The available phosphate deposits were considered to be important[359].

The Amman-al Salt line, which would help exploit the extensive phosphate deposits near al-Salt, was not built, mainly because the phosphate reserves were not as rich as expected. Meissner Pasha had estimated that the deposits held 1,000,000 cubic meters of phosphate, which the final report confirmed. Other large phosphate deposits in the region were not found worthy for working and transporting to the coast. Therefore, extending this

---

357 L/P&S/10/12, "From Mr. G. Barclay to Sir Edward Grey (Confidential)," Istanbul, 17 November 1906 in *IOR*.

358 L/P&S/10/12, "From Sir N. O'Conor to Sir Edward Grey (Confidential)," Istanbul, 12 June 1906 in *IOR*.

359 L/P&S/10/12, "From Mr. G. Barclay to Sir Edward Grey (Confidential)," Istanbul, 17 November 1906 in *IOR*.

branch line to Jerusalem was not feasible and crossing the rough terrain of Jerusalem cost too much. Estimates for the cost of working the phosphate deposits and selling them to European markets raised further doubts regarding the feasibility of the construction; therefore, transport and surveys were suspended[360] and work on the line was never started.

HAIFA—ACRE

As suggested, the short Haifa-Acre branch line would continue ten miles along the sandy shores of the Bay of Acre. Meissner Pasha reintroduced the plans for the branch line as a profitable endeavor. Preliminary plans were drawn up soon after, but its construction took a long time and proved difficult because the Nahr al-Mokatta, or Kishon, and the Nahr Namein, two rivers, complicated the construction, requiring costly foundations to cross over them[361].

AFULE—NABLUS

The Afule-Nablus sub-line would start from the Haifa-Deraa Branch, join the Afule-Jerusalem Branch in the Plain of Esdraelon, pass through Nablus, a well-populated, productive, and large town of Syria, and reach Jerusalem. The line was constructed without much difficulty, particularly because it followed the existing, main traffic line. Furthermore, the line was expected to significantly contribute to military purposes when it connected Jerusalem and the coastal towns of Jaffa and Ghaza to Damascus and greater Syria. This would allow Turkish troops quartered in Damascus to advance to Ghaza and confront the Egyptian frontier[362].

TEL AL-SHEMMAM—PLAIN OF SHARON JAFFA

The Tel al-Shemmam—Plain of Sharon Jaffa was another branch line that was planned to commence from Tel al-Shemmam on the Plain of Esdraelon,

---

360 L/P&S/10/12, "From Mr. G. Barclay to Sir Edward Grey (Confidential)," Istanbul, 17 November 1906 in *IOR*.
361 L/P&S/10/12, "From Mr. G. Barclay to Sir Edward Grey (Confidential)," Istanbul, 17 November 1906 in *IOR*.
362 L/P&S/10/12, "From Mr. G. Barclay to Sir Edward Grey (Confidential)," Istanbul, 17 November 1906 in *IOR*.

pass over a low ridge in eastern Carmel, and then arrive through the fertile Plain of Sharon in Jaffa. The line would be linked to Jerusalem and extend to Ghaza, if desired. This project was not fully outlined until 1906, especially since the Afule-Jerusalem line was the priority[363].

HAIFA—DERAA

The Hejaz Railway Project aimed to extend the railroad to the coast as fast as possible because the shipment of vast quantities of construction material via the French-owned Damascus-Beirut line was quite costly[364]. This objective led the Ottoman government to repurchase the concession previously granted. The government paid 150,000 Turkish liras for the concession, under the ownership of Mr. Arnold Hills of the Syrian Ottoman Railroad Company, and handed it over to the Hejaz Railway Commission[365].

The Haifa-Deraa branch line would link the following locations: Haifa, Shemamie, Nahr al-Mokatta, Tel al-Shemmam, Afule, Shatta, Beisan, Jisr al-Mejamie, Delhamie, Samakh, Yarmuk Bridge, Al-Hamme, Valley Khalid, Al-Shajara, Mukarram, Zeizoun, Tel al-Shehab, Muzeirib, and Deraa[366].

The construction of the Haifa-Deraa branch line began in Haifa soon after the British Company negotiated the matter. The line would run, as the initial British project proposed, from Haifa through the Valley of the Jordan into Damascus. However, the plan was changed with the railroad crossing the Jordan River in the town of Beisan, meeting the Sea of Gennesaret near Lamach, and then arriving in the deep and traditionally significant Yarmuk Valley and extending to Muzeirib[367].

Like the main line, the Haifa-Deraa branch line had a narrow gauge of 1.05 meters and its total length was 161 kilometers; 60 kilometers on the Plain of Zezreeh, 30 kilometers in the Valley of Jordan until the Lake of Gen-

---

363 L/P&S/10/12, "From Mr. G. Barclay to Sir Edward Grey (Confidential)," Istanbul, 17 November 1906 in *IOR*.

364 L/P&S/10/12, "From Mr. G. Barclay to Sir Edward Grey (Confidential)," Istanbul, 17 November 1906 in *IOR*.

365 L/P&S/10/12, "From Sir N. O'Conor to Sir Edward Grey (Confidential)," Istanbul, 12 June 1906 in *IOR*.

366 L/P&S/10/12, "From Mr. G. Barclay to Sir Edward Grey (Confidential)," Istanbul, 17 November 1906 in *IOR*.

367 L/P&S/10/12, "From Mr. G. Barclay to Sir Edward Grey (Confidential)," Istanbul, 17 November 1906 in *IOR*.

nesaret, 60 kilometers in the Yarmuk Valley, and the rest on the highlands of Hanran. From Haifa, at the zero kilometer mark, the railroad climbed 62 meters up Afule, stretched 36 kilometers, descended 246 meters to the Jordan Bridge, and crossed 76 kilometers to the Jisr al-Mejamie Station. From the Jisr al-Mejamie Station, the railroad inclined 187 meters in Samakh, 87 kilometers along the sea of Gennesaret, and then entered the very steep cleft of the Yarmuk Valley, via numerous bridges and tunnels. Near the Muzeirib Station, at the 149th kilometer, the railroad reached a height of 462 meters, which was the border of the Hanran Plain. The railroad, eventually, reached an elevation of over 529 meters at its final destination in Deraa, the 161st kilometer, with decent rises. Evidently, the advance of the railroad through the broken terrain of the narrow Yarmuk Valley, which had steep gradients, increased the costs considerably and presented overwhelming challenges for the construction. From Haifa to Jordan, very little masonry work was required for the greater part of the route allowing it to easily pass over the Plain of Jezreel. From Jordan onward, however, required great tasks of engineering: As the railroad approached the Yarmuk Valley, bridges, tunnels, and aqueducts had to be built one after another[368].

The line crossed over the Jordan with a massive, arched stone bridge that was simple in foundation but magnificent in appearance. Five, 12-meter wide arches spanned over the river. The maximum gradient was 20/1000 and the minimum radius for curves was 125 meters, except for some cases when the radius decreased to 100 meters. For the incline in the Yarmuk Valley, and for the sake of crossing it at various points, the geographical conditions made it necessary that two loops be made near the Seisun station into the tributary valleys of the Yarmuk. Therefore, two, 50-meter long bridges, four viaducts with one, 50-meter middle and two, 30-meter arches, were constructed completely from iron. In addition, a number of six to ten arched viaducts were built from stone over a span of 16 meters[369].

The construction of stone foundations required huge costs and two locomotives had to be bought for pumping operations. Eight, 1,100-meter

---

368 L/P&S/10/12, "From Mr. G. Barclay to Sir Edward Grey (Confidential)," Istanbul, 17 November 1906 in *IOR*.

369 L/P&S/10/12, "From Sir N. O'Conor to Sir Edward Grey (Confidential)," Istanbul, 12 June 1906 in *IOR*; and L/P&S/10/12, "From Mr. G. Barclay to Sir Edward Grey (Confidential)," Istanbul, 17 November 1906 in *IOR*.

tunnels were built. In the end, the last iron bridge was completed. Masonry and ironwork took a year and a half to conclude. Between 1 September 1901 and 1 September 1905, 65,000 cubic meters of stone work was finished on the Haifa section, while 30,000 cubic meters of stone work and 300,000 cubic meters of embankment were constructed on the Ma'an section, illustrative of the remarkable speed of the construction[370].

The Haifa-Deraa line, particularly its route through mountains and the Valley of Yarmuk, incurred overwhelming challenges. Half of the line's construction, from Haifa, was under the responsibility of Muhtar Bey, a Turkish engineer. The other, more difficult half, from the Lake Tiberias to Deraa, was divided into three main sections and contracted out. A significant part of the Hejaz Railway, contractors who were given these sections of the Haifa line were paid well enough to encourage them to do a good job[371].

The aforementioned viaducts required expensive labor and only locomotives could facilitate the pumping of the foundation's trenches. The bridges over the Yarmuk required more extensive use of iron than those on the main line, because they were built much higher above the bed of the valley, and in fact, iron was the best and cheapest material available and suitable for that purpose. There were a total of 83 bridges between Jordan and Muzeirib and on the Haifa line. Eight, 1,100-meter tunnels were also included in the construction efforts. Furthermore, the drainage in the Yarmuk Valley was crucial and represented a significant amount of work. In the end, the Jordan-Muzeirib section was composed of 246 aqueducts and culverts, while the section between Haifa and the Valley of the Jordan had only 56 culverts[372].

The Haifa railroad and the Hejaz's main line merged in Deraa. In these three sections, 1,200,000 cubic-meters of earthwork and 70,000 cubic meters of masonry work, in a period of fifteen months, were completed. Consequently, in October 1905, the entire line was ready for business, after the delayed steel bridges for the Yarmuk were delivered[373].

---

370 L/P&S/10/12, "From Sir N. O'Conor to Sir Edward Grey (Confidential)," Istanbul, 12 June 1906 in *IOR*.

371 L/P&S/10/12, "From Sir N. O'Conor to Sir Edward Grey (Confidential)," Istanbul, 12 June 1906 in *IOR*.

372 L/P&S/10/12, "From Mr. G. Barclay to Sir Edward Grey (Confidential)," Istanbul, 17 November 1906 in *IOR*.

373 L/P&S/10/12, "From Sir N. O'Conor to Sir Edward Grey (Confidential)," Istanbul, 12 June 1906 in *IOR*.

The following provides an overview of the cities and settlements situated between Haifa and Deraa[374]. Headings give the names of stations, distances between the stations, their kilometer on the line, and elevation in that order.

Haifa (+1.45)

Distance between the two stations: ---

Distance from the first station: 21.7

Haifa, the ancient Sycaminum and the seat of a provincial governor under the Mutasarrıf of Akka, was situated at the foot of Mount Carmel. Inhabited by 12,000 residents, Haifa was a lively trading center that mainly exported wheat, maize, sesame, olive oil, and wine. In particular, the German Templar Colonies on the slopes of Mount Carmel and the Jewish Colonies in the region cultivated large tracts of vineyards and processed wine for export. Half its population was Muslim and the other half was composed of Orthodox Greeks, Jews, Roman Catholics, Maronites, and Greek Uniates. Approximately 600 Germans dominated the European population of the region. There were not many wells, but those available provided an adequate supply of water. The station in Haifa had repair shops, one engine shed that was large enough to maintain eight engines simultaneously, one turntable, a water tank, and a pump that supplied water from a well, which was just north of the station. The station's 350-yard siding faced the dock. The railroad line passed along the foot of Mount Carmel and was parallel to the Nazareth Road. An extensively cultivated plain was located to the north of the station.

Shemamie (+39)

Distance between the two stations: 21.7

Distance from the first station: 14.6

Tel al-Shemmam was a fellaheen village of approximately 100 inhabitants. It had a small, stone station building with no siding but had an adequate source of water. The Nazareth Road crossed the railroad in Shemamie, near Zahluk, and continued along some slight clay cuttings. The station building had a 600-yard siding that crossed the road to a few quarries at the foot of Carmel. Although the siding was idle and unattached to the station, it was possible to connect it and put it into use.

---

[374] L/P&S/10/12, "War Office to Foreign Office," 26 July 1907 in *IOR*.

Bridge over Nahr Al-Mokatta

The line crossed over the Nahr al-Mokatta, or Kishon, by a 20-foot arched stone bridge. The stream below was 25-30 feet wide and 1.5 to 2 feet deep in the spring, and virtually dry in the summer. Here, the railroad followed the steep, rocky slopes of Carmel to the south and the spurs of the low wooded hills of Al-Harithie to the north. Then, the railroad reached the wide, Merj Amir Plain, or the Plain of Jezreel or Ezdraelon. The land in the region had fertile black soil that was well cultivated.

Tel al-Shemmam

Distance between the two stations: ---

Distance from the first station: 22

Tel al-Shemmam had a stone station building with a 250-yard siding. The rail tracks over the plain became very heavy after every rainfall. An unmetalled track was laid toward Jaida along the Nazareth Road.

Water Station

Distance between the two stations: ---

Distance from the first station: 32

At this location there was a 25 cubic meter water tank supplied by a pump through a deep, clay cutting for 200 yards.

Afule (+ 62.4) 206 feet

Distance between the two stations: 36.3

Distance from the first station: 14.7

Afule was a fellaheen village of an estimated 1,500 residents. Approximately 15 kilometers to the south was an ancient site, named later as Megiddo, where the German government led a series of excavations. Afule had a stone station building with a 300-yard siding, and a goods shed. A partially metalled, paved road crossed between Jenin and Nazareth together with three telegraph wires that extended between Jerusalem and Nablus. Wells provided a good source of water for the station in Afule and the villages were not far. The railroad crossed through a small watershed between the Mediterranean and a depression in Jordan. The rail tracks were functioned well in all directions across the plain when the weather was dry, however they were creaky and dysfunctional when it rained. The plain that the line passed over had marshes.

Shatta (- 78.19) 260 feet

Distance between the two stations: 51.0

Distance from the first station: 8.0

Shatta was a Fellaheen village of approximately 800 inhabitants who lived on the broad, orange-colored slopes a quarter of a mile to the north of the station. The station building was stone and had a 300-yard siding and water tank that was supplied from the Dadi Djalab Valley, a large area of well-cultivated land a mile away.

Beisan (-121.72) 398 feet

Distance between the two stations: 59.0

Distance from the first station: 17.3

Beisan, the old Canaanite town formerly known as Bethcean, was re-named Cally Senthopolis after the Seythian settlers who immigrated to the region. Three thousand residents populated Beisan and had a local governor. The Arabs of Beisan were not Bedouin but settled and civilized. Near various large springs was a large village, one mile north of the station. Tel al-Hisn, a fortress settlement, was the town's oldest section. The hills around the town hosted the ruins of a Hellenic, Roman town, that included bridges, a Roman theatre, arcade, and hippodrome. Tel al-Hisn was, also, surrounded by defensive falls and there was a large cemetery in the hill to the north. In addition to Hellenic, Roman ruins, Beisan had Byzantine monuments and inscriptions that dated back to the time when it was the seat of a bishop. Gardens flourished thanks to abundant irrigation. The vicinity around the town, up to the Tiberias Lake, was included on the Sultan's Civil List, the list of settlements. Beisan had a two-storey, stone station building with a 300-yard siding. The railroad exited the Zezereel Plain just after the Beisan station and entered the boundary of the Jordan Valley. The line descended into a well-cultivated valley with some small streams, which led to the wide Jordan Valley, and then curved to the north on unmetalled tracks with gradual declines and 1/100-1/150 gradients.

Jisr al-Mejamie Station (-246.47) 809 feet

Distance between the two stations: 76.3

Distance from the first station: 10.5

In Jisr al-Mejamie, just before the Jordan Bridge, there was a stone station building with a 300-yard siding and a water tank that was supplied from the Jordan. An estimated 200 local inhabitants lived in the area. An unmetalled track passed close to the station toward the Jordan Bridge. A large number of rails and steel sleepers were piled up near the station.

Jisr al-Mejamie Bridge (845 feet)

Distance between the two stations: ---

Distance from the first station: ---

There was a station over the Jordan that had six, 40-feet masonry arches, 12 meters each. The riverbed was rocky. A road bridge stood half a mile up the stream and was supported by a 40-foot stone arch.

Jisr al-Delhamie

Distance between the two stations: ---

Distance from the first station: ---

The railroad paralleled the left bank of the Jordan, through various, small clay cuttings, and embankments. It crossed the Sheriat-ı Menadere, or the Yarmuk River near the Jordan, over stone abutments, approximately 45 feet high with a span of 165 feet or 50 meters. Here the stream flowed through a narrow and rocky rift 200 yards below a series of small waterfalls. In fact, the bridge's maintenance was very difficult when necessary. A crossing where the hills end faced the Jordan and was 1,200 yards away. The Road Bridge, an old masonry with a number of irregular stone arches, that was 300 yards upstream, had been partially eroded by water and with time.

Delhamie

Distance between the two stations: ---

Distance from the first station: ---

The rail tracks passed to the left of the Delhami village of fifty dwellings, and then moved on through some small clay cuttings to the open, cultivated Jordan Plain. The Jewish settlement of Bukaa was visible from the railroad, 1.5 miles to the left at the bottom of hills.

Samakh (-186.88) 665 feet

Distance between the two stations: 86.9

Distance from the first station: 8.5

Samakh, located on the southern shore of the Tiberias Lake, or Bahr-i Tabaria or the Sea of Gennesaret, was an important station and had a large railroad depot before the long incline to the Yarmuk Valley. Landing was provided for steamer connections between Tiberias and Tapka in Samakh. It

had a two-storey station building, an engine shed for two engines, a turntable, a coal-loading stage, a small coal depot, and a goods shed. The station
had a 10-yard long loading platform and four, 400-yard sidings. Approximately 5,000 steel sleepers and 1,000 rails, which were stacked at the south
side of the station, were waiting to be shipped. The drinking water provided
by the lake was of high quality, and there was a 2.25 cubic-meter water tank
fed by water cranes and a steam pump on the edge of lake. In the Samakh
village there were 150 houses and 500 residents, mostly Algerian emigrants
and local Arabs who carried out some cultivation activities. The station's
wood landing stage was 50 yards long. A steam-launch with twenty-five passengers could reach Tiberias in 1.5 hours. Sailboats and rowboats also operated in the area. Along the shore, the tracks provided the wheels with easy
passage. In summer, there was a ferry service from Bab al-Tum that crossed
the Jordan. The line moved from the plain to the mouth of the Yarmuk Valley. While the railroad workers called the location Yarmuk, locals called it
Sheriat-ı Menadere. The mouth of the valley was very narrow due to the
steep hills on both sides. A river flowed through a narrow, rocky bed with
40 to 50 foot-high cliffs. The line skirted the right and north of the banks
that were made of white clay and soft rock.

2nd Yarmuk Bridge

Distance between the two stations: ---
Distance from the first station: 92
The line crossed to the left bank over an iron girder bridge of three
spans on stone piers, 40 feet above the water. The central span was 165 feet,
or 50 meters, and a lattice girder, with a span of 98 feet, or 30 meters, was
on both sides. There were also four stone arches of 20 feet, or six meters,
next to the left bank. The bridge was named the Second Yarmuk Bridge,
since the Hejaz Railway authorities named bridges in numerical order.

3rd Yarmuk Bridge

Distance between the two stations: 1
Distance from the first station: 93
The line then crossed the upper bend of the same loop and one kilometer higher was a third, similarly constructed bridge. This bridge was distinct
because it did not have stone arches next to the left bank. In addition, there
were basalt and white rock cliffs on the right bank, below the bridge.

Al-Hamme Station (476 feet)

Distance between the two stations: 2

Distance from the first station: 95

Al-Hamme Station consisted of a short building with a 250-yard siding. Hot springs of al-Hamme were on the far side of the bank, and the Umkeis village was situated on a knoll a mile and a half to the south.

Hamme (-146.06) 476 feet

Distance between the two stations: 95.3

Distance from the first station: 21.1

The Hejaz Railway owned sulfur springs in Hamme, which were a valued commodity during the ancient Roman era. The village of Kukes, or Roman Gadara, was 300 meters above ground level and 80 minutes away. The village had two Roman amphitheatres and miscellaneous Roman ruins, such as a public bath. Yarmuk river provided sources of water to the location, which the Bedouins inhabited in about thirty tents.

4th Yarmuk Bridge

Distance between the two stations: 1

Distance from the first station: 96

The railroad crossed to the left bank at the eastern end of the loop, over an iron girder bridge. Similar to the previous bridge, its central span was 165 feet and two others measured 98 feet and were built near the stone piers. The bridge was 30 feet high. The riverbed cut the slopes open and facilitated passage.

5th Yarmuk Bridge

Distance between the two stations: 4

Distance from the first station: 100

The railroad crossed to the right bank over an iron girder bridge. Like others, its central span was 165 feet and two others were 98 feet. The line passed along the right bank cutting a steep slope.

1st Tunnel

Distance between the two stations: 5

Distance from the first station: 105

Approximately 280 yards in distance, the First Tunnel was made of soft rock and shale, and it was completely lined with stone. The tunnel passed through a rocky spur, overhanging the river. The numbers were the names of the tunnels, which were written on the keystones of the outside arches in Ottoman Turkish.

6th Yarmuk Bridge

Distance between the two stations: 1

Distance from the first station: 106

The Six[th] Yarmuk Bridge was a stone bridge with six, 40-feet, or 12-meter, arches. The valley was a little wider in this zone. And the rails were 20 feet above the water.

Valley Khalid[375] Station

Distance between the two stations: 1

Distance from the first station: 107

The Valley Khalid Station had a small station building with a 250-yard siding that was in the open. With no villages nearby, Bedouins only occasionally visited the springs in the area. A number of paths led toward the valley's side. The left bank of the Mouth of Valley Khalid was close to the station. The line continued along the foot of a steep slope.

7th Yarmuk Bridge or Al-Kuye Bridge

Distance between the two stations: 7

Distance from the first station: 114

The Seventh Yarmuk Bridge was a stone bridge supported by five, 40-foot, or 12-meter, arches out in a small, open loop. There were very sleep slopes on either side of the main valley. A number of pathways led to the nearby plateau.

Sea Level

Distance between the two stations: ---

Distance from the first station: 116

The line remained at sea level here, out of the Jordan depression.

---

375 It is very likely that the Valley Khalid was named after the famous Muslim commander Khalid ibn Walid, who gained a decisive victory against the Byzantines at the Battle of Yarmuk in 636.

Al-Shajara Station (89 feet)

Distance between the two stations: 5

Distance from the first station: 119

Al-Shajara had one small station building on the steep slopes. The building had no siding but a steep foot track. The closest settlement was a village on the plateau four kilometers away[376].

Shajara (+26.89)

Distance between the two stations: 119.5

Distance from the first station: 5.1

Shajara was approximately four kilometers from a fellaheen village of 500 inhabitants with the same name. In addition, there were many other small villages and farms in the vicinity. Water was supplied from the Jarmak, 300 meters away[377].

8th Yarmuk Bridge

Distance between the two stations: 2

Distance from the first station: 121

The Eighth Yarmuk Bridge was a stone bridge with seven spans of 40 feet, or 12 meters, over a ravine that was usually dry. The bridge piers in the center were 35 feet high[378].

9th Yarmuk Bridge

Distance between the two stations: ½

Distance from the first station: 121.5

The Ninth Yarmuk Bridge was a stone bridge of five, 40-feet, or 12-meter, arches, and allowed the railroad to cross from the left bank of the river.

Mukarram Station (+71.14) 236 feet

Distance between the two stations: 11.2

Distance from the first station: 125

Mukarram, or the "junction of three valleys", had a small station building with a 250-yard siding out on a small, open plateau. There were no near-

---

[376] L/P&S/10/12, "War Office to Foreign Office," 26 July 1907 in *IOR*.

[377] L/P&S/10/12, "From Mr. G. Barclay to Sir Edward Grey (Confidential)," Istanbul, 17 November 1906 in *IOR*.

[378] L/P&S/10/12, "War Office to Foreign Office," 26 July 1907 in *IOR*.

by settlements and Mukarram was the closest station to the surrounding villages of Harta, Al-Rafid, Sahem al-Kafaret, Ekeir, etc.

10th Yarmuk Bridge

Distance between the two stations: 2

Distance from the first station: 127

The line crossed the right bank just above the junction of the Valley Ahrar over the Tenth Yarmuk Bridge, which was supported by three stone arches of 40 feet, or 12 meters, with a span of 20 feet, or 6 meters, at both ends.

2nd Tunnel

Distance between the two stations: 1

Distance from the first station: 128

After 250 yards, through the steep spur of soft white rock, the line reached the Valley Ahrar. It made a long loop there and climbed up to the Fourth tunnel, an addition to the Second Tunnel in the same spur that was a little further east.

11th Bridge

Distance between the two stations: ½

Distance from the first station: 128.5

The railroad crossed the right bank of the Valley Ahrar over a stone bridge with three arches of 40 feet, or 12 meters. The piers of the bridge were 25 feet above the rocky river bed.

12th Bridge

Distance between the two stations: 1½

Distance from the first station: 130

The railroad crossed the left bank of the Valley Ahrar, at the top of the loop, over a stone bridge with three spans of 10 feet, or 12 meters, and then inclined to a steady grade.

3rd Tunnel

Distance between the two stations: 1

Distance from the first station: 131

After an approximately 200-yard, inclined slope of the Valley Ahrar, the Third Tunnel was in a spur of white colored rock and had stone linings.

4th Tunnel

Distance between the two stations: 1

Distance from the first station: 132

The Fourth Tunnel was a curved tunnel of 280 yards in the same spur as the Second Tunnel, only higher. Here, the line returned to the Yarmuk Valley while the slopes ascended, and there was a steep cutting with a wall of rock on the north side. Rocks often fell on the rails, closing the line and blocking traffic.

Zeizoun Station (+260.19)

Distance between the two stations: 13.3

Distance from the first station: 136

Zeizoun, or Seisun, was a fellaheen village with an estimated 200 residents. In Zeizoun, a small station building stood on a sloped hillside led by steep tracks. The land was fertile in the region with a waterfall, water tank, and an adequate supply of spring water from the village on the plateau that was directly above the station, while a tributary of the Jarmak provided the land with irrigation.

5th Tunnel

Distance between the two stations: 1

Distance from the first station: 137

Through a spur of 250-yard long, soft rock, the Fifth Tunnel had stone linings.

6th Tunnel

Distance between the two stations: 1

Distance from the first station: 138

The Sixth Tunnel passed through a 300 yard long spur and had stone linings.

13th Yarmuk Bridge

Distance between the two stations: 2

Distance from the first station: 140

The line crossed to the left bank of the river, just under Tel al-Shehab village and waterfall, over a large bridge of iron girders and stone spans with one central span that stood 165 feet high. The lattice iron girder was below the rail level, with three, 40-foot, stone spans at the abutments on both sides. The line climbed up the Valley Meddan, made a long loop, and then reached Tel al-Shehab village, which overlooked the bridge. The steepest gradient was measured at this loop.

14th Bridge

Distance between the two stations: ½

Distance from the first station: 140.5

The line crossed to the right bank of the Valley Meddan, over a stone bridge with one central span of 40 feet, and three other spans that stood at 20 feet on both sides. The pier of the Fourteenth Bridge was 35 feet high. And the line continued, cutting up the side of the valley.

15th Bridge

Distance between the two stations: 2

Distance from the first station: 142.5

After a sharp-curved loop crossed the valley, there was the Fifteenth Bridge on the line. Standing over the rocky river bed, the bridge had one central span of 40 feet and spans of 20 feet on both sides.

7th Tunnel

Distance between the two stations: ---

Distance from the first station: 142.75

Soon after the Fifteenth Bridge, the line entered the Seventh Tunnel through a 120-yard curve. The other side of the loop ascended the line and there were several cuttings in soft rock and clay.

Tel al-Shehab

Distance between the two stations: 2½

Distance from the first station: 145

The line soon reached its maximum elevation as it approached the Hanran Station near the Tel al-Shehab Village. A little further to the north, there were 100 dwellings and a good spring water supply. The Hanran Station had a 250-yard siding and a small station building.

Muzeirib (+461.60)

Distance between the two stations: 11.8

Distance from the first station: 149

Previously, Muzeirib was a center of pilgrimage caravans, with a large bazaar. The village was divided into two sections with approximately 800 inhabitants. Kom al-Muzeirib, the island village, was built on an ancient site with a lake rich in fish. Dekakim, a relatively newer village located to the north, stood above the ruins of Qal'at al-Jedid, a fortress built by Turks. In the east was Qal'at al-Atika, an old fortress built by Sultan Selim I. Muzeirib had one stone station building with a 250-yard siding. The 25 cubic-meter water tank was filled by the Muzeirib Lake, one mile away to the north, with the help of a steam pump. Muzeirib station served as a connecting branch to the French line, which, about one mile long, was interrupted for a short distance. Half a mile further east, the pilgrimage route to Mecca intersected with the station.

Deraa

Distance between the two stations: 12

Distance from the first station: 161

In Deraa, the railroad merged with the Hejaz Railway main line.

OTHER LINES AND INTERSECTIONS

The Hejaz Railway Project considered the option of constructing half a dozen lines in association with the main line. The lines considered were named the Haifa Harbor Project, the line from Ma'an to Aqaba and Amman-al-Salt, the line between Jeddah and Mecca, a conjunction between Baghdad and the Hejaz Railroad that connected to the lines of Syria, the Central Anatolian Line, and the Riyaq-Beirut line[379].

THE HAIFA HARBOR PROJECT

Contrary to the findings of the initial proposal, later estimates concluded that the construction of a port in Haifa would be very expensive. The port, which was built at a distance of approximately 350 yards to a water depth of 15 feet, served to land the railroad material and stores from lighters. The port was made of rough, stone blocks that were quarried nearby; however, the structure could not withstand the northwesterly storms that hit the bay.

---

[379] L/P&S/10/12, "From War Office to War Office (F.R. Maunsell, Major, R. A.)," 27 July 1907 in *IOR*.

Therefore, the tail end of the port, which was 30 yards long, was washed away and the twisted iron rails showed the strength of the waves. As a result, building a breakwater was deemed necessary in order to shelter the landing quays. The proposed breakwater would be close to the town's front. Its A/B arm would spread 700 meters and then the breakwater would curve towards C, while the north side, next to the Bay of Acre, would form the main entry. The B/C arms would be built over a period of time so that the costs would not hinder the overall budget of the railroad. The A/D quay would extend 500 meters and 18 feet deep. The A/B and B/C arms would have landing platforms for large vessels and the rails along the port would be separated by 28 to 34 feet of water, which would support the facility. In addition, a considerable part of the gap would be filled-in, the only possible solution to the enlargement of the port, and warehouses and railroad sidings would occupy the space opened. The estimated costs reached 800,000 liras. However, as noted earlier, the construction of the entire breakwater would progress over time. When completed, the total cost for the breakwater would be 1,100,000 liras. Meissner Pasha strongly recommended that the port should be constructed and owned by the Hejaz Railway, instead of being leased to a foreign company for one main reason:. If a foreign company leased the port, it would compete with the Beirut Harbor and the consequence of which would be reflected in the rates, to the detriment of customers. So, it was more advantageous to keep it as state property[380].

THE LINE BETWEEN JEDDAH AND MECCA

Constructing a line between Jeddah and Mecca became even more urgent with time. The difficulties in constructing a line far from the seaport could be solved by establishing a branch between Mudawwara and the Gulf of Aqaba and between Jeddah and Mecca. The operational costs of the Haifa Harbor were considerable under bad weather conditions; and, also, it was too distant of a base. The delay in building the critically important Jeddah branch likely resulted from the fact that it would interfere with local camel traffic. Reportedly, the Sultan, himself, was strongly against the idea of having the railroad built close to the shores because he thought that the railroad

---

[380] L/P&S/10/12, "From Mr. G. Barclay to Sir Edward Grey (Confidential)," Istanbul, 17 November 1906 in *IOR*.

would be prone to naval enemy attacks. At any rate, linking the main line with the Red Sea was vital and it seemed that the foundation of the line was going to be built in the near future. Auler Pasha noted that the main cause in the delay of construction was due to financial problems. However, the construction expenses of the line between Jeddah and Mecca would be balanced with the opening of traffic on the projected line and the significant amount of income it would generate. Furthermore, the construction of this branch line would make sure that the Hejaz Railway's main line would take approximately three years, instead of five years.

The survey of the Jeddah-Mecca line indicated that there would be no engineering difficulties[381]. The line would follow the pilgrimage route and mainly serve pilgrims sailing from India and other destinations. Likewise, building a line between Yanbu and Medina was not too intricate and would produce a good source of income[382]. At the time the plans were set, however, the reaction to the line by the people engaged in camel trade was vague: doubts stemmed from the fact that the railroad would adversely affect Jeddah since pilgrims would no longer pass through there[383]. Whereas linking Mecca to the port in the Red Sea was not too expensive or complex, building junctions between Deraa and Haifa, and Ma'an and Aqaba, which would link the trunk line to the sea, was perceived as too costly and complicated to undertake[384].

The engineer, Ahmed Muhtar Bey, suggested that such a line could be built at a gradient of 20 millimeters with 300-meter curves with a total length of 75 kilometers[385].

Each kilometer of the line required 5,000 cubic meters to embank, 100 cubic meters of stone to construct, and 1,000 cubic meters of ballast to carry. Two battalions of 600 men could carry out the embanking, constructing, and ballasting in eight months; the endeavor would cost 15,000 francs per

---

381 L/P&S/10/12, "From Sir N. O'Conor to Sir Edward Grey (Confidential)," Istanbul, 12 June 1906 in *IOR*.

382 L/P&S/10/12, "From Mr. G. Barclay to Sir Edward Grey (Confidential)," Istanbul, 17 November 1906 in *IOR*.

383 L/P&S/10/12, "Sir N. O'Conor to Sir Edward Grey," Istanbul, 18 February 1908 in *IOR*.

384 L/P&S/10/12, "From Sir N. O'Conor to Sir Edward Grey (Confidential)," Istanbul, 12 June 1906 in *IOR*.

385 L/P&S/10/12, "From Sir N. O'Conor to Sir Edward Grey (Confidential)," Istanbul, 12 June 1906 in *IOR*.

kilometer, or 1,125,000 francs in total. In addition, the following costs remained outstanding:

Cost of the line (francs)	1,125,000
General expenses for one year	200,000
Two stone bridges and three reservoirs	200.000
Initial outlay for the Port of Jeddah	125,000
Railroad material	N/A
Ballast, 20.000 francs/kilometer	1,500,000
Four 30-ton locomotives	100,000
Fifty 16-ton wagons at 4,000 francs	200,000
Fifteen wagons at 16,000 francs	240,000
Total	3,750,000

The project's estimated cost was 50,000 francs per kilometer; furthermore, Ahmed Muhtar Bey's comprehensive estimation concluded that passenger and goods traffic would yield a profit of approximately eight percent, once the line opened[386].

In the report, submitted to the General Commission in Istanbul, regarding the railroad's inspection in autumn 1905, Geheimer Baurat Kapp von Ghrulstein, an authority in the eastern railroad construction, emphasized these considerations and suggested a plan accordingly.[387].

According to Kapp von Ghrulstein, two major tasks were necessary in order to complete the Hejaz Railway. First, the end of the main line from Damascus, which had reached 590 kilometers by 1 January 1906, should continue to Medina, a total of 1,400 kilometers, and then to Mecca, a total of 1,800 kilometers. Second, the Jeddah-Mecca section should be built so that the railroad's construction could have two starting points. This way, another construction could lead to Medina from there.

1. At the current rate of construction, an average of 150 kilometers per year, the would be finished up to Medain Saleh, a total of 360 kilometers, in approximately two years, by 31 December 1907; reach Medina, a total of 800 kilometers, in an estimated five years, by 31 December 1910; and even-

---

[386] L/P&S/10/12, "From Sir N. O'Conor to Sir Edward Grey (Confidential)," Istanbul, 12 June 1906 in *IOR*.

[387] L/P&S/10/12, "From Mr. G. Barclay to Sir Edward Grey (Confidential)," Istanbul, 17 November 1906 in *IOR*.

tually arrive in Mecca, a total of 1,200 kilometers, in approximately eight years, by 31 December 1913.

2. If construction on the line between Jeddah and Mecca, which was seven kilometers, started in 1906, the entire line would be finished by September 1907. Between 1908 and 1910, 100 kilometers of rail between Mecca and Medina could be laid and by the end of 1910, this newly constructed line could connect to the Hejaz Railway's main line that extended from Damascus.

As a result, the Hejaz Railway could finish three years earlier while the main line would have another outlet to the sea, through the connection provided by the Jeddah-Mecca line. In addition, the building of the Jeddah-Mecca section would be relatively easy: the gradients would not exceed 10/1000 and the curves would not be below a radius of 300 meters. Kapp von Ghrulstein further estimated that the Jeddah-Mecca line, including rolling-stock and station buildings, would cost 3,750,000 francs, a lower budget than previously calculated, due to the assistance promised by Turkish troops: A total of 1,000 soldiers had been assigned to the construction. Considering that 7.5 million francs, the annual income of the Hejaz Railway, had been spent on the construction of the main, Damascus-Mecca line, which advanced 160 kilometers a year, the General Commission would be forced to find other sources of income or take loans to build the Jeddah-Mecca line and extend it to Medina. Justified by the fixed income the General Commissioners took from the Ottoman Government in the form of stamp duties and other methods, Kapp von Ghrulstein believed that a loan would be profitable. Furthermore, von Ghrulstein gave the following calculation as firm evidence that the Jeddah-Mecca line would pay back the loans withdrawn:

A hundred thousand residents were living in and around Mecca and their food supply came to Mecca only by way of Jeddah. With a customs tariff of 0.05 francs per ton/kilometer charged on 300 kilograms of food per person every year.

The transport would generate an annual income of 1,500 francs. Assuming the number of pilgrims from Jeddah to Mecca at a minimum of 30,000, a fare of 0.10 francs per kilometer back and forth would yield 0.20 francs x 30,000 = 6,000 francs. The total income would be 7,500 francs. With 3,000 francs, the operating expenses per year/kilometer subtracted from the income, von Ghrulstein's calculation showed a surplus of 4,500 francs.

The calculated sum pointed to a net income of 3,750,000 francs, or eight percent. In fact, six to seven mejidiyes (Turkish liras, 50-60 piasters for a one-way trip between Jeddah and Mecca) charged to pilgrims was not excessive, considering that the return ticket price - 2.75 x 0.10 = 15 piasters - was added to the overall cost of the trip. In addition, the travel expenses of an average pilgrim could be doubled or tripled with the addition of one Turkish lira, the amount that was asked as a contribution to the construction fund of the Hejaz Railway. Taken cumulatively, the annual income of the Jeddah-Mecca section would increase from 13,000 to 43,000 liras. For pilgrims, the pilgrimage trip would be very comfortable, and inexpensive. In the absence of curves on the line, it would take two hours, at 40 kilometers/hour, for twelve, high-quality trucks to take 480 pilgrims from Jeddah to Mecca. Three, 30-ton locomotives, 50, high-quality, 15-ton trucks, and 15 passenger wagons, the operating costs of which were included in the total cost of 3,750,000 francs as "the rolling-stock on thin line", were all what was necessary for the trip. Three trains—the high-quality trucks would board third-class passengers—would shuttle back and forth, making four round trips a day. At this rate, they would carry 5,760 pilgrims from Jeddah to Mecca on a daily basis. In the end, that many pilgrims would reach their destination via the rails in a matter of one week. Furthermore, Kapp von Ghrulstein outlined the following reasons for justifying the importance of the construction of the Jeddah-Mecca line:

1. The broader Muslim world that was following the pilgrimage route from Jeddah to Mecca were those who had generously contributed to the Hejaz Railway. Yet, they would not benefit from the railroad that was under construction north of Medina. Therefore, the construction of the Jeddah-Mecca line would be just to these generous donors and give them solid proof that their donations were valued and would remain so in the future, as well.

2. The Jeddah-Mecca line would open a new outlet to the sea for the Hejaz Railway, which would facilitate transport trains carrying construction material to Medina, a total of 1,500 kilometers, and Mecca, a total of 1,900 kilometers. The transportation of construction material to the two cities presented a huge expense: transportation costs to Medina would amount to

7,950 francs (106 tons x 0.05 franc x 1,500) and to Mecca 10,070 francs (106 x 0.05 x 1,900). Therefore, it would be more advantageous to split the construction of the Damascus-Mecca line into two sections. The line, a total of 1,200 kilometers, was still under construction by 1 January 1906 and the southern half of the Jeddah-Mecca line was about to begin. Construction of the 400 kilometer-long railroad between Mecca and Medina could be started from the southern end, which would save three years in the construction of the entire Hejaz Railway, providing diplomatic advantages and increased morale. Foreign policy considerations had to be minimized and the profound significance and completion of the Jeddah-Mecca line would trigger the advancement and rapid completion of the main Damascus-Mecca line. These considerations, mentioned in the proposal drafted by Kapp von Ghrulstein, pointed to great and obvious advantages to come with the Jeddah-Mecca line and met approval by the authorities. They further testified that the work already progressing rapidly on the main Damascus-Medina line would gain greater momentum with this line[388].

By 1 January 1906, the main line would have reached the 590th kilometer. Damascus–950 kilometers to Medain Saleh, 1,400 kilometers to Medina, and 1,800 kilometers to Mecca–gave the following data:

The construction, which began in January 1901 when Meissner Pasha arrived in Damascus, reached the 590th kilometer of the trunk line and the 160th kilometer of the Haifa section, a total of 760 kilometers by 1 January 1906 with an average of 150 kilometers of rail laid per year.

The remaining work as of January 1906 is below:

Section	Length (km)	Period (years)	Completion date
	360	2	1 January 1907
Medain Saleh	800	5	1 January 1910
	1,200	8	1 January 1913

It was not easy to calculate the average expenditure per kilometer of the Damascus-Ma'an and Haifa-Deraa lines because some parts of the Haifa section would progress on uneven ground, requiring supplementary outlays.

[388] L/P&S/10/12, "From Mr. G. Barclay to Sir Edward Grey (Confidential)," Istanbul, 17 November 1906 in *IOR*.

Therefore, the average based on the total expenditure was not completely accurate[389].

MA'AN—AQABA AND AMMAN—
AL-SALT SUB-LINE PROJECTS

Strategically and economically, the construction of a branch line between Ma'an and Aqaba promised significant gains. The line would provide a direct link between Anatolia and the Red Sea and would eliminate the Ottoman Empire's dependency on the Suez Canal by establishing an independent communication route between the Ottoman provinces in Anatolia and the Arabian Peninsula. In addition, the overall cost of the line for the Turkish Government would not be too great in the long term, considering the fact that every vessel that passed through the Suez Canal was subject to pay a duty of 10 francs per ton. The railroad connection between Ma'an and Aqaba offered a strategic advantage since troops would be able to move much faster than by way of the Suez Canal, in case of an emergency in the Arabian provinces. As the events in the summer 1905 showed, the Syrian troops, which were needed to interfere in the unrest in Yemen, moved to Hodeidah in ten to eleven days, while it took two weeks for the Turkish troops to arrive via the Suez Canal[390].

Nevertheless, the construction of the Ma'an-Aqaba branch line was cancelled due to a border dispute between Turkey and Egypt and because the terrain presented overwhelming difficulties, adding to the overall expense of the construction[391].

The Ottoman Empire then looked for another outlet to the sea, south of Ma'an. Such an outlet was necessary not only for the reasons stated above but also, because construction material for the railroad and provisions for the troops and other laborers had to reach the construction site faster and more efficiently. The route via Haifa was too long; interruptions occurred while transporting goods and an excess of rolling stock caused an increase in expenses. Had the Hejaz Railway established a link between southern Ma'an

---

[389] L/P&S/10/12, "From Sir N. O'Conor to Sir Edward Grey (Confidential)," Istanbul, 12 June 1906 in *IOR*.

[390] L/P&S/10/12, "From Mr. G. Barclay to Sir Edward Grey (Confidential)," Istanbul, 17 November 1906 in *IOR*.

[391] L/P&S/10/12, "From U.F.S. to Foreign Office," Therapia, 6 August 1906 in *IOR*.

and the Red Sea, it would have been faster and cheaper to transport materials and provisions and the construction would have advanced more efficiently and rapidly. In fact, the rail line between Aqaba and Mudawwara was possible because the terrain between them was suitable for railroading. A branch line could also be established between Tabuk and Dhaba, also known as Siba, or between Tabuk and Muweila. Camel riders, according to the natives, covered the distance between Tabuk and Dhaba in two and a half days[392].

In lieu of a branch line between Ma'an and Aqaba, which was cancelled in 1906, there were three alternative routes[393]:

1. The first proposed line was a direct route between Ma'an and Aqaba through Guera, which would follow the track used by the troops. However, a sharp descent of an estimated 3,000 feet on the route from Ma'an to Guera would make the construction of this line very expensive; therefore, the authorities did not take this route into consideration.

2. A line originating further south, from Mudawwara to Aqaba, was also suggested. The line would start from the Valley Rutm Station, at the foot of the Batn al-Ghul descent, and follow a rough, but feasible, western route towards the Gulf of Aqaba. The line, according to Meissner Pasha, would extend 40 kilometers along the eastern shore of the Gulf, thus making it unlikely to be sanctioned by the Sultan.

3. A route from Ma'an that passed through the Valley Musa, the ruins of Petra, and a fairly easy and declining gradient into the Valley Araba, and all the way to Aqaba was also proposed. It seems that this route was the most feasible of the three routes under consideration. The construction would be the easiest and the rail lines would have natural protection from naval attacks. The route would cross an easy col toward Petra, but the following sections presented some potential engineering challenges, the decline into the Valley Arabah probably being the greatest[394].

A survey team went back to study the construction of a small branch line between al-Salt and a place yet to be determined on the main line be-

---

392 L/P&S/10/12, "From Mr. G. Barclay to Sir Edward Grey (Confidential)," Istanbul, 17 November 1906 in *IOR*.

393 L/P&S/10/12, "Consul Richards to Sir N. O'Conor," Damascus, 15 December 1903 in *IOR*; FO 195/2148, "Sir N. O'Conor to the Marquess of Lansdowne," Istanbul, 4 January 1904 and 29 December 1903.

394 L/P&S/10/12, "From Mr. G. Barclay to Sir Edward Grey (Confidential)," Istanbul, 17 November 1906 in *IOR*.

tween Zerqa and Amman. The study aimed to facilitate the exploitation of the phosphate deposits in al-Salt. Although the initial steps had been taken for this small branch line, the engineers were not asked to continue the mission and the construction of that branch was put on hold indefinitely. Pushing south from Ma'an, the line reached the Valley of Bactengoul in November 1905 and was completed up to Mudawwara in January 1906, which made a total of 572 kilometers of rail laid from Damascus[395]. The latter branch line project posed engineering challenges fewer than the line between Ma'an and Aqaba. Ma'an and Aqaba were approximately 110 kilometers apart but there were ground level variations up to 1,074 meters. Starting from Ma'an, the railroad would climb 1,600 meters in approximately 30 kilometers and decline in steeper gradients, after the Valley al-Araba, to the flat shore of the Red Sea. More precisely, the upper part of the valley descended 500 to 800 meters in only ten kilometers and this would require engineers to work on a gradient of 20/1000. The Ma'an-Aqaba line would cover 100-150 kilometers, the same length as the Haifa-Deraa branch line, and would cost the same as well. The construction of a branch line between Ma'an and Aqaba was cancelled; however, the idea still encouraged the authorities, particularly in surveying the region in order to construct a military route that would facilitate the transportation of troops. A hundred kilometers in length, with gradients that were not too high and a ten-meter radius on its sharpest curve, this military route would have advantages. When completed and supported by two stations offering water and barracks, the troops would be able to easily walk from Ma'an to Aqaba in three days. Later, the troops established the telegraph connection between Ma'an and Aqaba and a middle station; military telegraph clerks ran the telegraph centers[396].

Conjunction of Baghdad and Hejaz Railroads, and their Connection to the Syrian Lines

The political and military significance of the Hejaz Railway increased soon after it was connected with the Baghdad Railway. By the time the Anatolian

[395] L/P&S/10/12, "From Sir N. O'Conor to Sir Edward Grey (Confidential)," Istanbul, 12 June 1906 in *IOR*.

[396] L/P&S/10/12, "From Mr. G. Barclay to Sir Edward Grey (Confidential)," Istanbul, 17 November 1906 in *IOR*.

Railroad Company completed the Baghdad Railway up to Bulgurlu, at the foot of the Taurus Mountains, and the French Lebanon Railroad Company, the owner of the railroad between Damascus and Hamer via Riyaq, was ready to extend the railway to Aleppo. All that remained was connecting a gap between Bulgurlu and Aleppo so that a direct railroad could be established between Istanbul, Mecca, and the Red Sea[397].

In this respect, collaboration with the French Syrian Lines came under consideration. Despite apparent opposition, the joining of the French Syrian Lines with the Baghdad Railway was agreed upon, with the assumption that the government would offer more favorable terms. This arrangement would help the Baghdad Company garner high kilometric guarantees from the Syrian lines, especially on the section between Hama and Aleppo, and help pay for the heavy expenses of crossing the Taurus and Amanus mountain ranges. In light of recent negotiations, Meissner Pasha believed that the section between the Gulf and Mosul would rely on British capital, while the rest, between the Taurus Mountains and Mosul, would draw on French and German capital. Therefore, the French Syrian Lines merged with the Baghdad Railway. However, Meissner Pasha did not agree with constructing a port in Alexandretta, mainly because traversing the hills that looked over the town to the east would be very challenging; instead, the port could be built in Kestabol, in line with the Baghdad Railroad Concession. He knew that Kestabol was not an important city and was mentioned only in relation to Ayas or Yumurtalık, two famous sites a few miles away. Meissner Pasha strongly recommended that Tripoli be the main port in northern Syria; it had the best, well-sheltered harbor on the coast with a sandy bottom, which would require nothing more than dredging to reach the ideal depth. A smooth route could be found for the railroad on the busy road between Tripoli and Homs. There were no steep gradients and it could go around the northern end of the Lebanon Range easily. In addition, the gap between the Lebanon Range and the Ansarie Mountains provided access to the rich Plain of Homs and allowed an outlet to the coast for the broad gauged Aleppo-Homs-Riyaq line.

During the Baghdad Railroad Concession, the idea of constructing a branch line in Tripoli was a well-discussed idea. Furthermore, a line between Tripoli and Homs could be built cheaply. Meissner Pasha estimated that the

---

397 L/P&S/10/12, "From Mr. G. Barclay to Sir Edward Grey (Confidential)," Istanbul, 17 November 1906 in *IOR*.

total cost for this line, which would cover 95 kilometers between Tripoli and Homs, would be 150,000 liras, which excluded dredging the shores and the construction of a port in Tripoli. Meissner Pasha argued that the reputation and significance of the Port of Beirut were deceptive, a product of the events of 1860 that resulted in the creation of Lebanon as a separate province. For this reason, the potential of Tripoli as the main port of Syria was neglected. Meissner Pasha further argued that it was time to revive Tripoli and restore its proper status. Despite his persuasiveness on the matter, it would be too naïve to agree with Meissner Pasha on excluding Alexandretta as a port in the Mediterranean in association with the Baghdad Railway. In fact, Alexandretta was the natural port of Aleppo and other rich towns in the vicinity, while Tripoli was too far to the south to support these towns. The challenges related to traversing the hills in eastern Alexandretta were not too serious; to the contrary, surveys conducted after the British Company proposed the project noted that the entire construction would be quite feasible. Furthermore, the Baghdad Railway would traverse the same range, only higher, near Kazanalı, and face similar challenges to the other project to a certain point[398].

CENTRAL ANATOLIAN RAILROAD PROPOSAL

İzzet Pasha was quite interested in constructing an Anatolian line to connect Ankara, Sivas, Erzincan, and Erzurum. Similar to the Hejaz Railway, the Turkish Government wanted to undertake the construction of this line itself. Meissner Pasha noted that the project was offered to him and that he gladly accepted. The main objective of the line was strategic: a central Anatolian railway would fortify the Turkish national frontier defense in the northeast against a potential Russian attack from the Caucasus. The construction of this line would not negate the arrangements with Russia on railroad construction in the Black Sea basin, mainly because the lines constructed by the Turkish Government, not foreign companies, were exempt from the regulations stipulated in the agreement. When completed, the line would have facilitated the operations of the Ottoman army quartered in Anatolia, helping them move quickly across the Kars-Erzurum Route[399].

---

[398] L/P&S/10/12, "From Mr. G. Barclay to Sir Edward Grey (Confidential)," Istanbul, 17 November 1906 in *IOR*.

[399] L/P&S/10/12, "From Mr. G. Barclay to Sir Edward Grey (Confidential)," Istanbul, 17 November 1906 in *IOR*.

RIYAQ—BEIRUT LINE

Between Riyaq and Aleppo, there was only a broad gauge section and a narrow gauge section in Lebanon. As the present structure gave the broad gauge no outlet to the coast, it was proposed to construct a new line from Riyaq to Beirut. The new line would pass through a tunnel in Lebanon, decline down to the Valley of the Beirut River, and then reach the sea[400]. As the initial plan, the inventors of the rack-rail system were able to convince the company to accept it. At that time, the existing line was doomed to fail due to the traffic flowing from the interior and the improvements in Haifa and Tripoli, where nearly all traffic was diverted; therefore, a solution was necessary. Starting from Riyaq, the new, broad-gauge line would reach Zahle, follow the main ridge of Lebanon through a tunnel, approximately five kilometers long, and head to a tributary of the Beirut River, or Nahr al-Beirut. The line would run along the valley and around this river at a smooth gradient until it reached the sea in Beirut. In Beirut, the existing harbor did not function well; therefore, the proposal suggested a considerable extension to facilitate the increased traffic that was expected with the proposed scheme. The proposal further suggested carrying the broad-gauge line from Riyaq, through the Anti-Lebanon, to Damascus. Technically, this undertaking would be easy as the gradients along the way were not steep[401].

STATIONS AND THEIR CHARACTERISTICS

Damascus, Deraa, Amman, Qatrana, and Ma'an were the main stations on the Hejaz Railway. There were 27 stations along a total of 458 kilometers of the railway. The stations were built every seven to twenty-one kilometers between Damascus and Deraa and every 11-30 kilometers between Deraa and Ma'an[402].

---

[400] L/P&S/10/12, "From Mr. G. Barclay to Sir Edward Grey (Confidential)," Istanbul, 17 November 1906 in *IOR*; and L/P&S/10/12, "From Sir N. O'Conor to Sir Edward Grey (Confidential)," Istanbul, 12 June 1906 in *IOR*.

[401] L/P&S/10/12, From Mr. G. Barclay to Sir Edward Grey (Confidential)," Istanbul, 17 November 1906 in *IOR*.

[402] L/P&S/10/12, "From Sir N. O'Conor to Sir Edward Grey (Confidential)," Istanbul, 12 June 1906 in *IOR*.

Until 1907, no stations were built between Damascus, Medain Saleh, and Al-Ula. With one exception in Hamis, where a blockhouse was nearly finished, and other places had foundations laid and water cisterns constructed.[403] As a standard, the stations along the railway were provided with a large station building, engine-shed, turn-bridge, water tank, hydraulic crane, and a coal depot, as well as necessary sidings for the shunting of engines and wagons. In particular, workshops were built in Damascus, Deraa, Ma'an, and Haifa, while workshops were under construction at certain other stations.

While there was a decent dwelling to accommodate officials in Deraa, there was only a railroad house to accommodate seven officials, six workers, and one stationmaster, at other stations.

Water stations were erected every 30-70 kilometers, except for Amman in which the intervals between water sources were greater because of the absence of adequate water supplies. Wells or cisterns fed the water tanks. Steam pumps or wind pumps, which strong winds from the highlands occasionally interrupted due to the lack of trees, were the main equipment used to transfer water from sources to the tanks.

Unique to the Hejaz Railway, the passenger services included a number of lodges intended to accommodate passengers. All the station buildings were made of solid, hewn stone in a very simple fashion with tiled roofs. The stations were designed to run overtime at night[404]. The stone lodges covered an area of six to ten meters, similar to those on contemporary German military railroads. In particular, one lodge was reserved for the use of the stationmaster. The lodges were able to provide the modest needs of officials and passengers on the line past Oman[405].

Platforms to unload gun carriages and other equipment were not available at any station on the main or branch lines. Instead, gangways allowed the unloading of goods and materials at stations[406].

---

[403] L/P&S/10/12, "From Sir N. O'Conor to Sir Edward Grey (Confidential)," Istanbul, 12 June 1906 and 25 September 1907 in *IOR*.

[404] L/P&S/10/12, "From Mr. G. Barclay to Sir Edward Grey (Confidential)," Istanbul, 17 November 1906 in *IOR*.

[405] L/P&S/10/12, "From Sir N. O'Conor to Sir Edward Grey (Confidential)," Istanbul, 12 June 1906 in *IOR*.

[406] L/P&S/10/12, "From Mr. G. Barclay to Sir Edward Grey (Confidential)," Istanbul, 17 November 1906 in *IOR*.

People were not familiar with the railroad crossings, cabins, and barriers. Some caravans paid no attention to the official crossings when crossing the line. To prevent unwanted consequences, the cavalry detachments, which were quartered at a number of stations, patrolled the line occasionally and, also, served as watchmen.

Two units of infantry, mounted on camels, were assigned to guard the telegraph lines in the desert from Ma'an to Medina and to Aqaba. While they occasionally patrolled the line, some soldiers from the team examined and maintained the wires.

The great challenge for these infantry units stemmed from the fact that they had to patrol a wide area of 700 kilometers between Ma'an and Medina. This was complicated by the fact that intermediate stations were too few on the line, which exacerbated their work, including the inspection of wires.

A great number of workers involved in the construction had to be supplied with provisions. During the construction, passengers found and shared food along the way. When the construction finished and the workers left, the line's administration was compelled to include restaurant cars on their trains, as it would be clearly impossible to provide for the passengers in the desert[407]

Below are the station details between Damascus and Mudawwara (the stations indicated with asterisks are those having water sources)[408]:

Station Name	From Damascus in kilometers	Above sea level in meters
Damascus	0	+ 696
Kiswe	20	
Dair Ali	35	
Mismia	50	
Jebab	78	
Khebab	64	
Mehaye	92	
Ezra	104	
Kirbet-Ghazala	114	

---

407 L/P&S/10/12, "From Mr. G. Barclay to Sir Edward Grey (Confidential)," Istanbul, 17 November 1906 in *IOR*.

408 L/P&S/10/12, "From Sir N. O'Conor to Sir Edward Grey (Confidential)," Istanbul, 12 June 1906 in *IOR*.

Deraa	127	+ 520
Nessib	41	
Mafraq	166	
Hurbety-Samra	189	
Zerqa	208	
Amman	228	
Kassir	239	
Libban	256	
Jiza	269	
Deba'a	286	
Khan Zebib	301	
Qatrana	330	+ 783
Valley Sa'id	350	
EI-Hassa	383	
Zarouf	419	
Uneiza	464	
Ma'an	458	+ 1000
Aqaba	518	+ 1050
Batn al-Ghul	534	
Mudawwara	572	+ 734

The distances between Damascus and various stations are listed below[409]:

Station Name	Kilometers to Damascus
Abu Taba	1270
Al-Medina	1300
Amman	230
Uneiza (Anazie)	410
An Tabarah	1762
Afsan	1680
Badr al-Nabi Hasan	1460
Badr al-Ravishet	1425
Badr al-Saleh	1480
Bahra	1790
Batn al-Ghul	520

[409] L/P&S/10/12, Therapia, 6 August 1906 in *IOR*.

Bayar Tarif	1230
Badr al-Deriliski	1350
Buahad	1768
Damascus to Kiswe	18
Dar al-Hamra	870
Deba'a (Qal'at al-Deb'a)	270
Dair Ali	30
Deraa	120
Al-Hassa	365
Hadda	1785
Hadich	1125
Halis	1650
Jabal Abu Zerqa	910
Jabal Istabl Antera	1175
Jeddah	1830
Jeneyat al-Kadi	780
Jeradah	1803
Kadmie	1620
Qal'at al-Zerqa (Zerqa)	203
Qal'at al-Mudawwara	570
Qal'at al-Zumurrud	1030
Qatrana	315
Khan Zebib	940
Mustawere	1530
Ma'an	430
Mecca	1750
Mismia	50
Rabiah	1568
Rashamah	1817
Shakt al-Hajj	1370
Shemamie	1775
Tabuk	680
Valley Fatima	1720
Valley al-Muhasheme	820
Batn al-Ghul	720
Zat al-Hajj	600

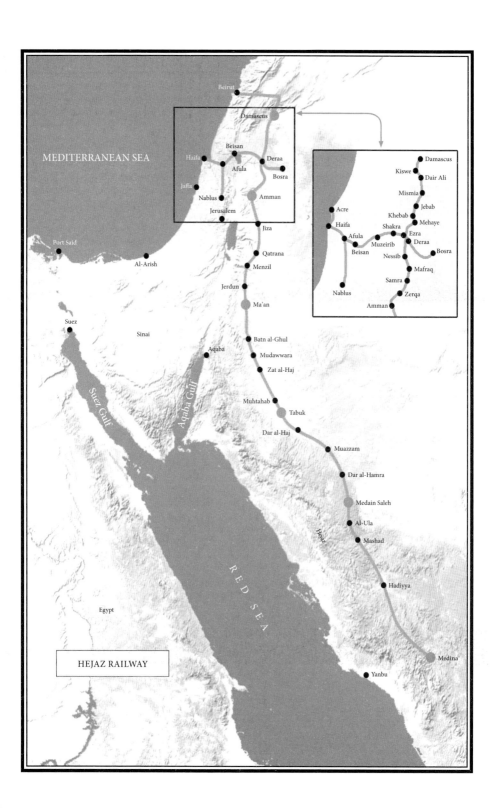

MEDITERRANEAN SEA

Beirut
Damascus
Beisan
Haifa
Deraa
Afula
Bosra
Jaffa
Nablus
Amman
Jerusalem
Jiza
Port Said
Qatrana
Al-Arish
Menzil
Jerdun
Ma'an
Suez
Sinai
Batn al-Ghul
Aqaba
Mudawwara
Zat al-Haj
Muhtahab
Tabuk
Dar al-Haj
Muazzam
Dar al-Hamra
Medain Saleh
Al-Ula
Mashad
Hejaz
Hadiyya
RED SEA
Egypt
Medina
Yanbu
Suez Gulf
Aqaba Gulf

Damascus
Kiswe
Dair Ali
Mismia
Jebab
Acre
Khebab
Mehaye
Haifa
Shakra
Afula
Ezra
Muzeirib
Deraa
Beisan
Bosra
Nessib
Mafraq
Samra
Nablus
Zerqa
Amman

HEJAZ RAILWAY

Sultan Abdulhamid II, the driving force behind the project

Baghdad railway, the line passing near Mosul

Sharif Hussein's son Amir Abdullah (left) meeting with Ronald Storrs (right) on the British ship Iron Duke

Maan was an important station on the Hejaz Railway

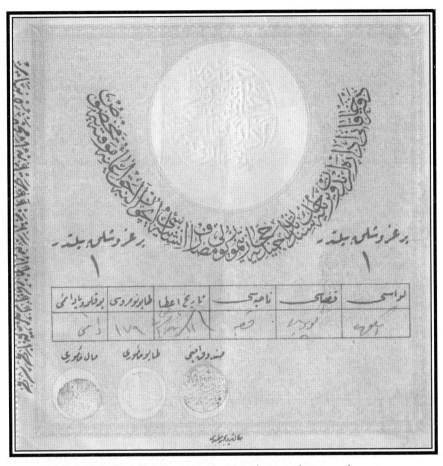

A 1-kurush receipt given in return for contributing to the construction of the Hejaz Railway

Sharif Hussein

The remains of the railway and the neighboring telegraph line in Jordan

Present view of the telegraph post in Damascus. There is a model of
the Hamidiye Mosque on top on the post

The Ottoman state emblem in relief on "Sutun al-Ali," Haif

Depiction of a train in marble relief on "Sutun al-Ali."

The locomotive numbered 4724, bought from Germany for the Hejaz Railway

The stone bridge at the 224ᵗʰ km of the Hejaz Railway

The cistern at the Shemamie station today

The stone bridge 20 km from Haifa

The head engineer Meissner Pasha

The Ottoman soldiers at the construction site near Tabuk

The opening ceremony of Muazzam station

Bedouins

The Ottoman cemetery near Haifa station

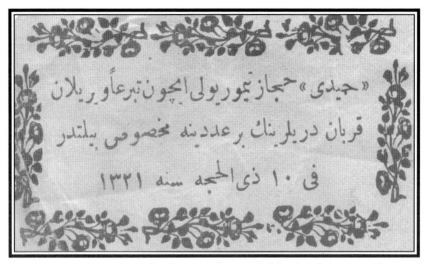

A receipt given in return for donation of an animal skin for the Hejaz Railway

The British agent T.E. Lawrence (third from right) talking to the pilot. The other men in the picture are British agents, Bedouins, and local Circassians

T.E. Lawrence

One of the symbols of the Hejaz Railway

"Sutun al-Ali" in Haifa is one of the still surviving memorials of the railway

Pilgrims brewing tea on the train

The first tunnel at the 104ᵗʰ km of the Hejaz Railway, not far from Haifa

Present condition of the Shemamie station

Maan station

An old locomotive near Israel-Jordan border

Street vendors at Homs station

*A medal given to those who made contributions to the
construction of the Hejaz Railway*

One of the special passenger cars used for praying

The trains at Khan Zebib

Even today one can see "Hejaz" written on some trains

Homs train station

The pilgrims on their way to the holy cities

Sketch of a locomotive for the Hejaz Railway

Pilgrims praying during a stopover

The end of the line in Medina

Cover of L'illustration magazine. The issue dated 3 Oct 1908 announced the arrival of the Hejaz Railway in Medina. The photograph shows Muhtar Pasha reading the Sultan's decree to the congregation

Final station of the Hejaz Railway in Medina

Construction of a bridge

The train halted at Ma'an for the Pilgrims to pray

Commemorative Stamps

PART FOUR

General Analysis

GENERAL ANALYSIS

ACHIEVEMENTS OF THE HEJAZ RAILWAY

Following the analysis of the Hejaz Railway, its rolling stock, and station details, this section examines the significance and achievements of the Hejaz Railway. It will be appropriate to begin with the military aspect, since the railway held a crucial role from the military standpoint. Thus, the analysis in this section will begin with the transportation of troops, particularly on the Damascus-Ma'an section, the shortest route to the Gulf of Aqaba, the Red Sea, and the Arabian provinces.

The longest distance between two stations on this section was between Jurf al-Derwish and Uneiza, at 25.3 kilometers. In absence of steep gradients in this zone, the average speed on the Hejaz Railway, which was 23 kilometers per hour, could be increased to 27 kilometers per hour. The return journey between Jurf al-Derwish and Uneiza, including the time necessary to change trains, took approximately two hours. The interval between trains leaving Damascus and those returning from Ma'an was fixed at two hours, which allowed ten military trains a day to leave Damascus at two-hour intervals. After the departure of the last train from Damascus, there was an interval of four hours. The following day, the same number of trains could set out from Damascus, while the first train returning from Ma'an reached Damascus by the evening of the same day.

The new locomotives on the Hejaz Railroad, which were 46 tons in weight, could haul 168 tons at a speed of 23 kilometers per hour. They had to slow down to 15 kilometers per hour only on the gradient in southern Amman. An eight-ton wagon loaded with 40 men weighed 12 tons. The number of wagons required to transport a battalion of 800 men are listed below:

For	Wagons	Tons
800 men, per wagon	20	260
60 pack animals, 6 animals per wagon	10	120
Ammunition	1	23
Tents	1	23
Luggage	1	23
Officers	1	23
1 luggage van for battalion officers	1	12
1 cistern wagon for train	3	105
Total	38	558

Since ten, 168-ton trains could make the trip from Damascus to Ma'an in one day; it was possible to transport three battalions on the same day, provided that the railroad and water supplies were sufficient.

The distance between Damascus and Ma'an was 458 kilometers therefore, the trip could be completed daily by taking one of the trains running at a speed of 23 kilometers per hour, including stops at stations and waiting on the sidings. Records of this type were made with the opening of the railway. For instance, on 30 August 1904, the participants of the opening ceremonies took five private trains, including one provision train, running at two-hour intervals from Damascus to Ma'an. Although each station gave the visitors official receptions, lengthening the regular stopping time, the first train arrived in Ma'an on the same day. In 32 hours, all the trains reached Ma'an. In the summer of 1905, 28 Syrian battalions that were assigned to quell the unrest in Yemen took the trains from Damascus to Ma'an with irregular intervals. In a day or two, all the trains they boarded reached their destination, with night stops extending the travel time. The troops moved from Ma'an to Aqaba, a distance of 110-120 kilometers, in four days, which was an outstanding achievement considering the fact that the terrain was broken and lacked proper roads. They sailed from Aqaba to Hodeidah, which took five days[410].

---

[410] L/P&S/10/12, "From Mr. G. Barclay to Sir Edward Grey (Confidential)," Istanbul, 17 November 1906 in *IOR*.

British Perspectives on the Construction

The British officials thought that the Hejaz Railway Project would suffer financial difficulties and harbored doubts regarding the ability of the Ottoman government to generate sufficient funds in order to sponsor the enterprise[411]. They had solid reasons: the project was massive in scope and the financial deficits were already challenging the Ottoman Empire's economic capacity. A railroad from Jeddah-Mecca—the project often contemplated and discussed—would be overwhelmingly difficult to construct and without sufficient funding. However, the Muslim community came to their aid with donations[412].

Although the British officials were pessimistic about the future of the project, they were interested, at the same time, in specific railroad proposals and were quite attentive to the voice of the Muslim world, including those in their colonies, like India[413]. For example, a British representative evaluated the information given by the local governor that the Muzeirib line would reach Amman in a matter of several weeks, Qatrana in nine months, and Ma'an within 18 months. He considered these estimates as "pious opinion"[414]. The British officials were confident in their beliefs that the execution of the Sultan's imperial edict to muster all the means available to complete the railway up to Medina, within a year, would bear no results. The edict, they thought, was imprudent and not worthy of being taken seriously[415].

The British officials, also, believed that the future progress of the construction would be far slower, mainly because the French Company refused to allow material for the construction of the line over the Beirut-Muzeirib railroad, under their ownership, if exorbitantly high rates were not paid as duty. Therefore, the Ottoman government decided to push the construction of the Deraa-Haifa branch at full speed so that this branch could transport the construction materials. In 1903, the British side began to reconsider their initial pessimistic approach towards the project, since the Ottomans were dedicated and progressing in taking the railroad to Medina and Mecca.

---

411 FO 78/5452, "The Marquess of Salisbury K.G.," Istanbul, 23 May 1900.
412 FO 78/5452, "Sir Nicholas O'Conor, G.C.B., G.C.M.G.," Damascus, 30 April 1900.
413 FO 78/5452, "The Marquess of Salisbury K.G.," Istanbul, 23 May 1900.
414 FO 78/5452, "From Sir N. O'Conor to the Marquess of Landsdowne," Damascus, 4 November 1902.
415 L/P&S/10/12, "W. S. Richards," Damascus, 8 February 1902 in *IOR*.

Former reservations and pessimism gave way to growing interest and they started to believe that the project was possible[416].

The British agents and councils wrote a number of detailed reports on the progress of the construction of the Hejaz Railway and its sections. Based on the reports, the British authorities began to think that at the present rate of progress it would be possible to finish the project in ten years[417].

Realizing that the project had a future, the British authorities studied the diplomatic and military aspects of central Arabia in association with the coming of the railroad. For instance, they believed that if the Turks wished to establish a line base to move into central Arabia, they had to choose Tabuk or Akhdar as the starting point for such an expedition, because water was not available, particularly in Muazzam, the nearest point to Hail. In order to succeed, the Turks had to alter their present system, more efficiently organizing supplies for their columns in the long, desert marches, and establish communication lines that the mobile enemy forces could not raid. Turkish troops were usually successful in open warfare, but the problem of maintaining supplies and communication was their Achilles' Heel. Thus, an inland movement from Tabuk or Muazzam towards central Arabia was a far more difficult operation than would appear from simply working out distances on a map and required a better system of organization, which the Turks lacked until then[418].

Beyond their anxiety and interest in the Hejaz Railroad, some British representatives submitted alternative routes for the Hejaz Railroad considering the possibility that the line could be used against the British forces in Egypt. For example, one British representative, an expert in the Hejaz Railroad, proposed constructing a line to link Egypt and the Euphrates Valley in Nejef, where it would join the proposed Baghdad line. The line would connect rich Egypt and fertile Mesopotamia. It would follow the ancient route between Egypt and Assyria, which passed though the rock city of Petra, the old capital of Edom. From Cairo, the line would run near the Suez and across the Sinai Peninsula, heading to the Gulf of Aqaba. Then, the line would climb towards Ma'an, through Petra, which had good supplies of water along the way, particularly in Petra. From there, the line would cross the Valley Sirhan, across a stony des-

---

[416] L/P&S/10/12, "Consul Richards to Sir N. O'Conor," Damascus, 15 December 1903 in *IOR*.

[417] L/P&S/10/12, "W. S. Richards," Damascus, 8 February 1902 in *IOR*.

[418] L/P&S/10/12, "From Mr. G. Barclay to Sir Edward Grey (Confidential)," Istanbul, 17 November 1906 in *IOR*.

ert, where there were no hills to hinder construction. This section lacked water, but there were decent wells in Hudruj and wells could be dug to provide supplies of water at other points. The line would reach a fair supply of water when it reached the Valley Sirhan. Jerouf was an important oasis on the northern edge of the Great Nefud Desert, which was, consequently, avoided. The oasis in Jerouf had 50,000 inhabitants, mainly in Skaka and Kara. On the Euphrates, between Jerouf and Nejef, the route would be built in the wide depression of al-Udian, which was a fertile pastureland and where there were several wells that the Bedouins of the Roalla and Aneize tribes used. Problems regarding water would only be incurred on a short section between Ma'an and the Valley Sirhan, however it was possible to build wells. The line would be almost entirely dependent on traffic between the two countries. However, Mesopotamia would assume a high level of development after the lower section of the Baghdad Railway opened, irrigation projects commenced, and a considerable amount of commercial activity entered the region. The line would be the most direct route from Bussorah and Lower Mesopotamia to Egypt, avoiding a long sea passage from India to the Mediterranean. The proposed line was composed of the following distances:

The distance from Cairo to Ma'an, through Aqaba and Petra, was 305 miles, or 492 kilometers; Ma'an to Jerouf was 260 miles, or 420 kilometers; Jerouf to Nejef was 310 miles, or 500 kilometers. The total distance between Cairo and Nejef was 875 miles, or 1,412 kilometers, a little longer than the distance between Damascus and Medina, which was 1,300 kilometers. The construction of the line between Cairo and Nejef could simultaneously start in Aqaba, Ma'an, Nejef, and Cairo. Each kilometer on the line would cost 1,400 liras and the total expenditure to build the whole line would be 3,000,000-3,500,000 liras, all inclusive[419].

Transportation and the Hejaz Railway

The British were aware that the successful completion of the magnificent Hejaz Railway would bring great prestige to the sultan[420]. No work of this

---

419 L/P&S/10/12, "From Mr. G. Barclay to Sir Edward Grey (Confidential)," Istanbul, 17 November 1906 in *IOR*.

420 L/P&S/10/12, "From Sir N. O'Conor to Sir Edward Grey (Confidential)," Istanbul, 12 June 1906 in *IOR*.

caliber had been carried out in the Muslim World since the early rise of Islam[421]. It was likely that the diplomatic and military significance of the Hejaz Railway would increase when it was linked with the Baghdad Railway sometime in the future[422]. The first train arriving in Mecca heralded a dawn of prosperity in the Arabian Peninsula[423]. In these and other respects, the railway was a remarkable and praiseworthy enterprise[424].

By the time the Anatolian Railroad Company completed the Baghdad Railway up to Bulgurlu, at the foot of the Taurus Mountains, and the French Lebanon Railroad Company, the owner of the railroad between Damascus and Hamer through Riyaq, was about to extend the railway to Aleppo, all that remained was a gap between Bulgurlu and Aleppo. With its completion, a direct railroad between Istanbul, Mecca, and the Red Sea would be established. The delay in Riyaq was a serious matter in terms of transporting troops. At this station, the typical gauge line originating in Istanbul changed to a narrow gauge, which required unloading and reloading horses, carriages, and war material. The change in the size of the gauge and transferring rolling stock required a change in speed. After the junction of the two railroads in Bulgurlu, the smaller trips on the Istanbul-Mecca line took the following periods of time:

Travel line	Distance in kilometers	Hour/s
Istanbul-Bulgurlu	918	60 kms = 15.8
Bulgurlu-Aleppo	510	50 kms = 10.2
Aleppo-Riyaq	332	60 kms = 5.5
Riyaq-Damascus	60	23 kms = 3
Damascus-Mecca	1,800	23 kms = 78.5
Total	-	113

Including seven hours of stopping time, the total trip took 120 hours, or five days. Delays, such as reloading in Riyaq, increased the time necessary

---

[421] L/P&S/10/12, "From Sir N. O'Conor to Sir Edward Grey," Therapia, 18 September 1907 in *IOR*.

[422] L/P&S/10/12, "From Mr. G. Barclay to Sir Edward Grey (Confidential)," Istanbul, 17 November 1906 in *IOR*.

[423] L/P&S/10/12, "From Sir N. O'Conor to Sir Edward Grey," Therapia, 18 September 1907 in *IOR*.

[424] L/P&S/10/12, "From Sir N. O'Conor to Sir Edward Grey," Therapia, 18 September 1907 and (Confidential) Istanbul, 12 June 1906 in *IOR*.

to transport troops to approximately six days. In eastern Jordan or the Hejaz, there were no major industries at the time. Salt deposits were discovered in Wadi Sirhan, near the foot of the spurs of the volcanic Hanran Mountains, near Kef and Etseri; however, they were only partially and ineptly extracted by the residents of nearby villages. Camel caravans took the extracted salt to Damascus, which was in high demand because of its high quality. In the broader region of Hanran and Adjling, there were sulfur deposits and oil wells. In addition, undefined and unused amounts of iron and other ores were discovered. In the Adjling district, near Jedar, there were large quarries of large and good quality millstones. The coming of the railroad, it was expected, would promote the exploitation of these valued minerals. The ancient Roman mines in the area, Midian, were mostly in ruins at the time of railroad's construction, but promised rich deposits of silver and, especially, turquoise. The arrival of the railroad would probably restore the activity of these mines. Otto von Kapp Kohlstein outlined the income that would be generated in the future:

Annual income of the Haifa-Deraa-Damascus section and, also, the Deraa-Amman section, which was a total of 385 kilometers, would barely exceed 3,000 francs per kilometer. The Haifa line, in the wild valleys of the Yarmuk and Jordan, would contribute nothing and the section on the plain of Jezreel would contribute little, because of the competition posed by camel caravans near the sea. The entire income, therefore, had to come from the Hanran and this income would have to be shared with the Muzeirib-Damascus line. The income might suffice to cover the operational costs. All of the long section that was south of Amman would, however, offer no income worth mentioning. The Mecca pilgrims travelled free of charge and the few tourists who would travel every year to Petra via Ma'an would make no substantial difference. The line south of Ma'an was to be regarded as a purely military railroad and it was planned to hand over its operation to railroad battalions with only one train a week. With such a limited amount of traffic, the expenses could be covered with 1,500 francs per kilometer, which made a yearly outlay of 2.5 million francs for the 1,600 kilometers under consideration. Since at least some of the taxes created for the payment of the construction of the Hejaz Railroad could still be levied after the completion of the railroad, there was no reason to fear that the enterprise would come to an untimely end for a lack of funds[425].

LAUNCHING THE RAILWAY

The completed sections of the line were launched without waiting until all of the construction was finished. On 1 September 1904, for instance, the Haifa-Jordan section was officially opened to traffic. On 1 September 1905, the Jordan-Muzeirib section was opened and became the first Turkish railroad connection with the Mediterranean. In May 1907, the main line was introduced to traffic up to Tabuk, 693 kilometers away from Damascus, while the trains used for construction were simultaneously running to Qal'at al-Akhdar, 761 kilometers from Damascus[426]. In addition, 237 kilometers, or 148 miles, of the Damascus-Amman section was put into operation. There were five carriage trains and two passenger trains running back and forth every week. The profits began to steadily increase: the lowest estimate of total income per month was 600 Turkish liras, while higher estimates reached a total income of 2,000 Turkish liras per month. An average estimate predicted that the income generated from the railroad was 1,000 Turkish liras a month[427]. In early July 1908, the railroad between Yanbu and Medina was also opened with the passage of three to four large merchant caravans[428].

The Damascus-Ma'an line, which was 458 kilometers in length, was another section opened to traffic. On the anniversary of the Sultan's accession to the throne, a ceremony was held to celebrate the occasion and the opening of the Damascus-Ma'an line by a special imperial mission, which was led by the Minister Tarhan Pasha. The following is a brief overview of the ceremonies held when the lines opened:

On 30 August 1904, the guests of the ceremonies boarded five private trains, including a provision train that left Damascus for Ma'an, at two-hour intervals. Because of the official receptions given at each station, the expect-

---

425 L/P&S/10/12, "From Mr. G. Barclay to Sir Edward Grey," Istanbul, 17 November 1906 in *IOR*.

426 L/P&S/10/12, "From Mr. G. Barclay to Sir Edward Grey," Istanbul, 17 November 1906 in *IOR*.

427 L/P&S/10/12, "Consul Richards to Sir N. O'Conor," Damascus, 15 December 1903 in *IOR*.

428 FO 195/2286, "Acting British Consul, Charge de Affaires," Istanbul, 30 July 1908.

ed time of arrival was delayed; the first train reached Ma'an 24 hours after its departure. Within 32 hours, all trains reached their final destination. On 1 September 1900, a grand ceremony was held, with a high turnout, to celebrate the completion and opening of the sections of the Hejaz Railway that spanned between Damascus and the city of Tabuk, which was a total of 692 kilometers. This was a special day for the entire Muslim world because it was the day that the Caliph-Sultan rose to the Ottoman throne. All the guests paid a visit to the Holy Mosque of Tabuk, early in the morning, and performed their *fajr* prayers, the Muslim prayer at dawn, led by the Müfti of Damascus, who was the leading preacher of Islam. Prayers were recited for the Sultan's precious health. At the end, the visitors marched in front of the standing imperial troops and entered the large tent that was established behind an impressive looking arch. There, the band played the Hamidiye March and the celebration ceremony was held with refreshments and coffee. During the occasion, 21 cannons were fired to celebrate the day. The retiring soldiers of the battalions involved in the construction were given their medals, wages, and tezkéres (discharge certificates) and then all the battalions took part, with the cavalry detachments joined by some Bedouin cavalry, in an impressive military demonstration. Quite a number of Arabs, sheikhs, and Bedouins, from Medina and Syria came to Tabuk and prayed for the Sultan. Attendees congratulated each other throughout the day and, at 9 pm, the visitors travelled two kilometers outside of Tabuk, where they helped to carry crossbars. The Imperial troops took up the rest of the work and laid 1,200 meters of rail in two and a half hours. Later, the visitors headed back to Tabuk, sacrificed sheep, and ate at a table with rice, meat, desserts, and refreshments. All the shcikhs and Bedouins were generously served, as were the troops and other visitors. At night, the city was marvelously illuminated with thousands of lanterns; shots were fired in the air with blank bullets, and the passion and enthusiasm outlasted the night. Prayers for the well being of the Sultan were continuously heard; the visitors left for Haifa early the next morning and returned to Damascus the following day[429].

The imperial commission, which left Istanbul to participate in the opening of that section of the Hejaz Railway, arrived in Damascus on 22 September 1906. After staying five days in the city, the commission set out on a five-

---

429 L/P&S/10/12, "War Office to Foreign Office, (Report of the Major Maunsell, R.A. on the H.R.)," 27 July 1907 in *IOR*.

day journey, on 27 September, aboard two trains destined to Medain Saleh and Al-Ula. They participated in the ceremonies, the first event in the reports, to celebrate the opening of the line and anniversary of the Sultan's accession to the throne. This activity took one day and they returned to Haifa soon after. Specifically, the commission was composed of Ferik Auler Pasha, Ferik Cevat Pasha, İsmail Hakkı Bey, and Ali Nuri Bey, the last two were sons of the Turkish Foreign Affairs Minister. Müşir Kazım Pasha, the Minister of the Hejaz Railway Construction, Müşir Ali Rıza Pasha, the Minister of Transportation, Abdurrahman Pasha, Muhafız al-Hajj, and approximately 100 dignitaries and officials accompanied them on the way to al-Ula. From there, the commission travelled to Beirut, Aleppo, and Erekli back to Istanbul[430].

For the celebration of the Tabuk line, the trains that carried the Imperial Commission and other distinguished guests left Damascus for the Tabuk station, with prayers and well wishes. With an enthusiastic welcome by an impressive gathering of people, the commission arrived in Tabuk on 18 August 1906. Early in the morning, the members of the ceremony committee got dressed into their uniforms and went to the mosque for the *fajr* prayer with tribal leaders, local notables, intelligentsia, and merchants.

After the lively ceremony, all the attendees walked along the rails that had been constructed; two kilometers of rails took a mere two hours for the entire group. Walking the rails made them more appreciative of the troops who constructed them. The night was beautifully illuminated and cannon balls were fired five times during this great celebration, keeping the spirit alive. The celebration committee left for Haifa the next day[431].

The last opening ceremony for the Hejaz Railway was held when the entire railway was completed. Selected delegates, approximately a hundred men, departed Mecca for Medina to attend the last grand opening ceremony for the Hejaz Railway. Chosen from all classes and communities of Mecca, the delegates were sent off by the Sharif of Medina, Mecca, and Jeddah to attend the opening ceremony of the Hejaz Railway between 11 and 12 September 1908[432]. In addition, the Sharif, scholars, preachers, governors, and

---

430 L/P&S/10/12, "Sir N. O'Conor to Sir Edward Grey," Istanbul, 25 September 1907 in *IOR*.

431 L/P&S/10/12, "War Office to Foreign Office, (Report of the Major Maunsell, R.A. on the H.R.)," 27 July 1907 in *IOR*.

432 FO 195/2286, "Acting British Consul, Charge de Affaires," Istanbul, 30 July 1908.

local notables joined the ceremony[433]. In the end, the Hejaz Railway was proclaimed, in the midst of great enthusiasm, launched. In September 1908, the operation of the Hejaz Railway's 1,300 kilometers of rail began[434].

IMPACT OF THE RAILWAY ON NEARBY DISTRICTS

The Hejaz Railway Project predicted that the railroad would revitalize regional commerce. However, it was later discovered that the challenges were too overwhelming for this to become a possibility. One of the major challenges was the difficulty in sound and safe communication between officers and workers. Some armed groups living near the railroad, between Deraa and Medina, blocked communications, harassed workers, and impeded the construction and flow of traffic as much as possible. According to an eyewitness account in Haifa, the Hejaz Railroad port, the rail lines were attacked 123 times in 1908, alone. They broke telegraph wires, dislocated rails, pillaged stations, and robbed wagons and passengers. In response to each attack, government officials remained composed: the officials compensated losses and repaired the railroad but they did not concern themselves with prosecuting the attackers, who escaped to the desert and could neither be tracked nor caught. Unfortunately, these outlaw mobs affiliated with certain tribes did not realize that the damage they inflicted would cost them dearly in the long term. The railroad, as the government aimed, was going to provide food to their people and wealth to their stagnating economies.

Commercial revival was not enough of an incentive for most settlements near the line, most being small, agricultural towns, as they did not anticipate an immediate economic boom in the near future. Even Medina had approximately 50,000 residents. The pilgrims, however, benefited immensely from the railroad and contributed large profits to the Damascus Province. In the year 1908 alone, over 10,000 pilgrims visited Damascus on their way back from the Holy Cities and gave the provincial market significant commercial activity and large profits from their shopping and purchases. If the line reached Mecca, Damascus could expect at least 10,000 pilgrims to visit

---

433 FO 195/2286, "Charge d'Affaires, (S. Mohammad Hasan, Jeddah)," Istanbul, 17 August 1908.
434 FO 424/219, "Sir G. Lowther to Sir Edward Grey," Istanbul, 5 April 1909.

per year; when the line connected Mecca and Jeddah, it was anticipated that the volume of trade for Damascus would rise considerably[435].

After the line's construction began, Circassian emigrants of several thriving villages began cultivating fertile lands in districts near Amman and in the Zerqa Valley; they succeeded in protecting their newly acquired lands. In addition, cultivation in the fertile Hanran district extended to the south, considerably, and east of Deraa, making it the most important revenue source for the railroad. Traffic from the fertile plain of Esdraelon (Merj Amir) on the Haifa branch continuously increased, despite the ongoing competition with local camel caravans. European tourists arriving via the Haifa line, from Nazareth and Tiberias to Damascus, provided another significant source of revenue. However, revenue was gained from the sections between Damascus and Amman and on the Haifa branch; the sections between Amman and Ma'an and the desert regions in southern Arabia generated practically no income for the line. Despite these shortcomings, in 1906 a revenue of 12, 000 Turkish liras was gained from pilgrim traffic up to Tabuk[436].

PUBLIC ATTENTION AND THE PRESS COVERAGE

The Imperial Hejaz Railway Project, specifically the idea of constructing a railroad from Damascus to Mecca, attracted public attention and received a good deal of media coverage in Istanbul[437]. Regardless of their social and economic status, Muslims were quite interested in the progress of the railroad's construction. Among the intelligentsia, there was also a sense of conviction, appreciation, and understanding that the Hejaz Railway would culminate in stronger diplomatic and military power[438].

The following quotation, from an issue of the Turkish newspaper *İkdam* published on 27 July 1900, further illuminates on the reception of the Damascus-Mecca rail line in the Muslim world:

---

435 FO 424/219, "Sir G. Lowther to Sir Edward Grey," Istanbul, 5 April 1909.

436 L/P&S/10/12, "From Mr. G. Barclay to Sir Edward Grey (Confidential)," Istanbul, 17 November 1906 in *IOR*.

437 FO 78/5452, "Sir Nicholas O'Conor, G. C. B., G. C. M. G.," Damascus, 30 April 1900; and FO 78/5452, "H. R. O'Conor," Istanbul, 23 May 1900.

438 L/P&S/10/12, "From Mr. G. Barclay to Sir Edward Grey," Istanbul, 17 November 1906 in *IOR*.

In all parts of the world Muslims vying with one another in their eagerness to contribute to the great work of the Hejaz Railroad which has been started by his Majesty the Sultan. Private advices from Bombay state that the Muslims of India will contribute with the greatest joy and gratitude and have already begun to apply to the Ottoman officials there and present their subscriptions, thus affirming the obvious spiritual bond which unites them to the Caliphate and showing their readiness to acknowledge it[439].

In addition, remarkable ceremonies were held in honor of the Hejaz Railroad and the completion of its various lines. A number of articles in Turkish newspapers and broader public attention throughout the Ottoman Empire focused on such ceremonies, especially on the progress of the lines, the challenges met, and the great significance of the entire railroad enterprise. In the confidential letter below, Mr. G. Barclay informed Sir Edward Grey of the future construction plans and the warm reception the Hejaz Railway received from the Muslims at the reception:

...This extraordinary work, accomplished in such a short time, was self-speaking-evidence of the numerous successes of His Imperial Majesty the Sultan. It was to be hoped also, that the remaining portion of the Hejaz line, which stands so high and sacred before the eyes of all the Muslims, will happily reach an end very soon, so that the pilgrims within reach of these facilities will be able to go and pray in those holy regions. Was it possible to conceive any other religious service more sublime than this? The whole Muslim nation was naturally proud of the accomplishment of such a super human and sacred work of our illustrious sovereign, work, accumulating in itself all the greatest, religious, and non-religious, advantages. Its moral advantages, besides the advantages of securing, at the same time, the welfare of all the faithful there, were beyond inception. This huge line, which is to surpass 2,000 kilometers, will revive and immerge into prosperity and wealth all those regions... Remarkable also is the extraordinary speed exhibited since the beginning of the construction of the Hejaz line, because the distance from Damascus to Tabuk, requiring all the way along bridges, tunnels, and lots of other things, which of course require time; thanks, nevertheless, to the praiseworthy measures taken by His Imperial Majesty, everything attained its end with extraordinary rapidity. Every single person hopes, and

---

[439] FO 78/5452, "Marquess of Salisbury K. G.", Therapia, 27 July 1900.

most sincerely wishes, that such a noble work, attracting both God's satisfaction and the Prophet's contentment, should be accomplished as soon as possible. It is quite obvious that as the most important part of the great line was finished in a very short time, the remaining portion also, will attain its end before long[440].

[440] L/P&S/10/12, "From Mr. G. Barclay to Sir Edward Grey (Confidential)," Istanbul, 17 November 1906 in *IOR*; and newspaper extracts from *Ikdam*, 19 August (1 September) 1900.

CONCLUSION

While the construction of the Hejaz Railway intended to protect the political integrity of Syria and the Hejaz, the railway eventually challenged the involvement of European powers, namely Britain and France, in the region. The Ottomans predicted that the railway, when launched, would substantiate the legitimacy of Sultan Abdulhamid II's rule. Furthermore, the Damascus-Mecca line would provide the Ottoman Empire with a strong grip on the Hejaz through Sharmar and Kassir.

For the Muslim World, the Hejaz Railway Project was the most glorious and biggest enterprise since the early days of Islam. The connection of the Hejaz Railway with the Baghdad Railway attributed special political and military significance to the Hejaz Railway. And this would happen soon: the Anatolian Railroad Company completed the Baghdad Railway as far as Bulgurlu, on the skirts of the Taurus Mountains, and the French Lebanon Railroad Company, the operator of the railway from Damascus via Riyaq to Hamer, was extending the railroad to Aleppo. The only uncompleted section was from Bulgurlu to Aleppo. After its completion, all the lines would link, thereby establishing a direct railroad connection from Istanbul to Mecca and the Red Sea. Symbolically, the arrival of the first train in Mecca would signal the dawn of a new, prosperous era for the Arabian Peninsula. Therefore, it would be a worthwhile project in numerous ways.

According to the initial plan, the construction would rely on Ottoman labor and use domestic equipment. Foreign expertise would be sought, mainly, in the field of engineering. While foreign engineers were responsible for the administrative and technical aspects of the project, Ottoman soldiers labored on the construction. In fact, the Ottoman soldier labor force was crucial for the project, considering that even high salaries did not attract the needed manpower to work in the wilderness that the railroad would cross. By 1 September 1904, the soldiers had already carried 3,800,000 cubic meters of soil and their vital contribution made the construction far cheaper than preceding construction projects in Turkey.

The Hejaz Railway Project was intended to increase the Ottoman Empire's military power and fortify its political authority. The main objectives of the construction were not just to maintain governmental and administrative involvement in Syria and the Hejaz, but the railway also challenged European powers, namely Britain and France. In addition, the completion of this remarkable railway would confirm Sultan Abdulhamid II's rule.

Apparently, the Damascus-Mecca line was essential for Turkey to establish a strong and well-disposed network reaching to the Hejaz through Sharmar and Kassir. From the early rise of Islam to Sultan Abdulhamid II's accession to the Ottoman throne, no other work in the Muslim world was carried out in the caliber of the Hejaz Railway. The diplomatic and military significance of the railway would considerably increase as soon as it was connected to the Baghdad Railway. The Baghdad Railway, already completed up to Bulgurlu, located on the skirts of the Taurus Mountains, by a partnership with the Anatolian Railroad Company and the French Lebanon Railroad Company, which also owned the railroad from Damascus to Hamer via Riyaq, would soon stretch all the way to Aleppo. The single, remaining gap between Bulgurlu and Aleppo would have to be railed so that a direct rail line would link Istanbul with Mecca and the Red Sea. The first train reaching Mecca would herald the beginning of a new, prosperous era for the entire Arab world. Therefore, for a myriad of reasons, the Hejaz Railway was praiseworthy to the fullest extent.

The Hejaz Railway made it possible for the passengers to cover a distance of 1,200 kilometers in three days. The pilgrims took advantage of the comfort and reduced travel time that the railroad provided. With the pilgrims in mind, throughout the journey the prayer schedule was observed and a railroad car with an Imam, the religious leader in Islam, allowed them to pray together. Four years after the opening on 1 September 1908, the Hejaz Railway carried approximately 30,000 pilgrims from various routes to Medina, annually. As a result, pilgrims, who came to the region, revitalized business. By 1914, the annual number of travelers on the Hejaz Railway soared to 300,000 passengers, which includes non-pilgrims as well as pilgrims.

The Hejaz Railway Project emerged, essentially, as a diplomatic and religious enterprise. Interestingly, the following report from the Cologne Gazette published on 25 July 1907 summarizes, rather nicely, the objectives, current status, and future plans of the Hejaz Railway:

Commenced officially on 1 September 1900, the construction is going to be finished in seven short years and continue to advance from Damascus down south for about 850 kilometers. In judging on the average of work accomplished so far, the facts must be set straight: including the construction of the difficult Deraa-Haifa branch line on the Mediterranean, 101 kilometers, in three years between 1903 and 1906, seven years marked the expansion of railroad for 1,011 kilometers, with an average of 148 kilometers per year, an average that has closely matched Gehcimrat von Kapp's raw estimation of 150 kilometers a year. Mister von Kapp, under the Sultan's order, travelled the first part of the railroad and sent in a report dated 1901. In his report, von Kapp outlined the essentials of the organization in the later part of the railroad construction. In 1905, another report followed his second field-trip. His first report pointed to the immediate necessity of a rail-line with Haifa, and suggested that Ma'an and Aqaba be connected via rails, apparent challenges notwithstanding. First, a line between Ma'an and Aqaba would establish a strategical connection, and provide a vital link from Jeddah in the south through Mecca to Medina. Just the line in Haifa was constructed. The construction plan of Ma'an-Aqaba branch line, which an imperial edict sanctioned in the autumn of 1904, fell short in face of the diplomatic objections of the ambassador in Istanbul. Likewise, the plan to connect Jeddah to Mecca by constructing 75-kilometer rails fell short because certain groups in Istanbul were scared of a potential coup against Mecca before the rails in the north were set, letting Mecca be defended. At the same time, however, measures went into effect in starting foundations for a line from Mecca to Medina, in an effort to rapidly transfer materials, shipped from the north, from Medina to Mecca. Medina is about 1,450 kilometers away from Damascus, and Mecca about 1,850; in view of the distance, 500-900 kilometers of rails remain having to be built, as on 1 September 1907, as the end of the railroad is almost half-way to Mecca by now. The railroad can reach up to Medina in 1910, and Mecca three years later. The date of arrival of the railroad in Mecca could be shortened almost a year on condition that the foundations would be laid from Mecca to Medina in the coming three to four years. At any rate, the work accomplished is a praiseworthy effort. In any case, the Turks and other Muslims were convinced of its significance to donate large sums to the Hejaz Railway. On 1 September 1906, grand sums amounted to 57,000,000 francs, and it is likely that this amount will increase, during this year, about 10,000,000 francs more, which will eventually secure the financial status of the railway. The first hand and driving force behind this great work is, next to the Sultan, İzzet Pasha, the Sultan's Second Secretary and Chamberlain, who brought about the current success of the scheme due to his first-class competence, unrelenting working strength, and iron-made energy. Let it also not be forgotten that the construction's technical manager (the German engineer) Meissner Pasha, who pursued his entire career from a foreman to the chief engineer responsible for the railroads in Turkey under the direction of Geheimrat von Kapp, and never concealed his attachment to Turkey and her search in power at home and abroad, receives a great pleasant share of success in this great work, wishing it successfully finished without delays for internal or external reasons[441].

The construction of the Hejaz Railway stemmed from diplomatic, political, and religious motives. From the very beginning, the Hejaz Railway attracted the attention, excitement, and generosity of the greater Muslim community, thanks in part to the continuous global news flow. The main line's eventual arrival in Medina was an occasion for cheerful celebrations in the Muslim world.

Even though the Hejaz Railway did not operate for long, it had long-term consequences: a great number of railroad engineers, technicians, machinists, managers, and laborers gained and practiced first-hand skills in an expansive project. Strikingly, in a very short time, the Hejaz Railway changed its image amongst the public, assuming an Islamic connotation that remains until today. The reconstruction and operation of the Hejaz Railway could fulfill the project's original objective and provide possible solutions, perhaps even become "a Bridge of Peace", to the major problems of the Middle East.

---

[441] L/P&S/10/12, "From Sir F. Lascelles to Sir Edward Grey," 14 August 1907 in *IOR*.

BIBLIOGRAPHY

MAIN SOURCES

ARCHIVAL SOURCES

Indian Office Library and Records, Londra, Political and Secret Department,

London, England:

L/P&S/10/12, From Mr. G. Barclay to Sir Edward Grey, Confidential, Istanbul, November 17, 1906.

L/P&S/10/12, From Sir N. O'Conor to Sir Edward Grey, Confidential, Istanbul, June 12, 1906.

L/P&S/10/12, War Office to Foreign Office, July 26, 1907.

Foreign Office Archives, London, England:

FO: 195/2286, Acting British Consul. Charge de Affaires, Istanbul, July 30, 1908.

FO: 195/2286, Charge d'Affairs, Istanbul, (J.H.McMahan, Consul, Jeddah) August 17, 1908.

FO: 424/219, Sir G. Lowther to Sir Edward Grey, Istanbul, April 5, 1909.

FO: 78/5452, From Consul W. S. Richards to Sir N. O'Conor, November 10, 1902.

FO: 78/5452, Sir Nicholas O'Conor, G. C. B., G. C. M. G., Damascus, April 30, 1900.

REPORTS, TELEGRAMS, AND MEMORANDUMS BY

Nicholas R. O'Conor, Vice Consul, Therapia.

F. R. Mansell, Lt. Col., Istanbul.

J. N. Monahan, Damascus.

W.S. Richards, Consul, Damascus.

N. O'Conor to Marques of Landsdowne, Istanbul.

W.S. Richards to N. O'Conor, Consul, Damascus.

General Wilkiel Young, Consul, Syria.

Sir R. N. O'Conor to Sir Edward Grey, Istanbul.

Loiso, Vice Consul, Istanbul.

Mr. G. Barclay to Sir Edward Grey, Istanbul.

Telegram by His Excellency Rahmi Pasha, Aide – de – Camp of the Sultan, and a member of the High Committee of Military Inspection.

War Office to Foreign Office.

Sir F. Lascelles to Sir Edward Grey, Berlin.

G. P. Devey to Sir N. O'Conor, Consul, Damascus.

J. N. Monahan to Sir N. O'Conor, Consul, Jeddah.

Sir Gerard Lowther to Sir Edward Grey, Istanbul.

G. P. Devey to Sir Gerard Lowther, Consul, Damascus.

Sir Gerard Lowther to Sir Edward Grey, Istanbul.

J. N. Monahan to Sir Gerard Lowther, Consul, Jeddah.

Report on the Hejaz Railroad by Herr von Kapp Kohlstein.

Memorandum by Mr. G. A. Lloyd on Hejaz Railroad.

Report by Auler Pasha respecting the Hejaz Railroad.

Report on the Hejaz Railroad by Major R. A. Maunsell.

BOOKS AND OTHER REFERENCES

Books:

Eraslan, Cezmi; II. Abdülhamid ve İslam Birliği, İstanbul 1992.

Rüştü Paşa, Akabe Meselesi, İstanbul, 1326.

Khairallah, Shereen; Railroads in the Middle East 1856 – 1948 (Political and Economic Background), Librairie du Liban, 1991, (Lebanon).

Gülsoy, Ufuk; Hicaz Demiryolu, İstanbul 1994.

Engin, Vahdettin; "Osmanlı Devleti'nin Demiryolu Siyaseti", Türkler, Yeni Türkiye Yayınları, v. XIV, Ankara 2002.

Ochsenwald, William; The Hejaz Railroad, The University Press of Virgina, 1980.

Articles:

Eyyuboğlu, Emine; "Hicaz Demiryolu İnancın ve Emeğin Yolculuğu", PTT Dergisi, Ocak 2002, Ankara, Number 27.

Özyüksel, Murat; "Hicaz Demiryolu Türkler", Türkler, Yeni Türkiye Yayınları, v. XIV, Ankara 2002.

Öztürk, Said; "Hicaz Demiryolu", Osmanlı Devleti'nin 700. Kuruluş Yıl dönümünde Sultan II Abdülhamid Dönemi Paneli (II), Bilge Yayıncılık, İstanbul 2000.

Web Pages:

http://members.tripod.com/mirzabeyoglu/secmece153.htm

http://nabataea.net/hejaz.html

http://www.arab.net/saudi/sa_hejazrailroad.htm

http://www.balgawi.com/Jordan/History/Ottoman(Oman).html

http://www.golan.org.il/article1.html

http://www.kinghussein.gov.jo/his_Ottoman(Oman).html

http://www.railroadtouring.co.uk/body_july – dec_.html#Hijaz

http://www.trainsofturkey.com/history_over.htm

http://www.trainsofturkey.com/hist_over.htm

http://www.turkishmedals.net/others.htm#Hejaz

INDEX